D0984203

*Caught
in the Net*

Number Seven:
*Kenneth E. Montague Series in
Oil and Business History*

Caught in the Net

in the

The Conflict between Shrimpers and Conservationists

BY
Anthony V. Margavio
and Craig J. Forsyth

WITH
Shirley Laska and James Mason

TEXAS A&M UNIVERSITY PRESS
College Station

The paper used in this book meets the minimum requirements
of the American National Standard for Permanence
of Paper for Printed Library Materials, Z39.48-1984.
Binding materials have been chosen for durability.

This research was supported by the University of New Orleans
Environmental Social Science Research Institute
and the National Oceanic and Atmospheric Administration
Office of Sea Grant, Department of Commerce, under grant
No. NA85AA-D-SG141. The University of New Orleans Sea
Grant activities are a part of the Louisiana Sea Grant Program
which is administered by Louisiana State University.

Library of Congress Cataloging-in-Publication Data

Margavio, Anthony V., 1938–
    Caught in the net : the conflict between shrimpers and conserva-
tionists / by Anthony v. Margavio and Craig
Forsyth with Shirley Laska and James Mason. — 1st ed.
        p.   cm — (Kenneth E. Montague series in oil and
business history ; no. 7)
        ISBN 0-89096-669-9 (cloth : alk. paper)
        1. Shrimp fisheries—Environmental aspects— Southern
States.   2. Sea turtles—Southern States. 3. Wildlife
conservation—Southern States.   4. Shrimpers (Persons)—Southern
States—Interviews. 5. Conservationists—Southern States—
Interviews.   I. Forsyth, Craig J. II. Title.   III. Series.
SH380.62. U6M37   1996
333.95'7—dc20   95-37565
                                                          CIP

Contents

Illustrations

Preface

In the summer and fall of 1989, hundreds of shrimpers blockaded Gulf ports and waterways in protest of regulations designed to protect sea turtles. Today angry shrimpers continue to resist the regulations that mandate the use of turtle excluder devices (TEDS). Shrimpers' objections to TEDS have been that they are dangerous, do not work properly, and lose shrimp.[1]

This book tells the story of the conflict evinced by these regulations. It is not, however, just about changes in shrimping nor is it merely about how shrimpers managed to launch a protest of TEDS regulations. It is about marine resources: shrimp, fish, and turtles. It is about the difficulties and dilemmas government agencies face as they try to reconcile conflicting goals. And it is a story about environmentalists and the environmental movement and how they select their issues. It is a story of the oil and waste disposal industries and their relationships to commercial fishers. It is a story of state and local governments and why they choose sides in resource conflicts. It is a story of elites, their influence over the flow of capital, and their effects on land use patterns. It is a tale of the transformation of America's coasts from farming and fishing villages into recreational communities and the accompanying displacement of farmers and fishers. It is about the ambiguities and tensions of our conservation and environmental laws and how these tensions reflect unresolved national issues, particularly economic enhancement versus environmental protection. The TEDS conflict is also about power and ethics and how resource conflicts emerge and how they are resolved. It is about the resistance to and consequences of social change. It is a story of holding on to traditions in the face of great obstacles and about a world that has lost its way traveling the road of progress.

In the beginning of our investigation, we were caught off guard by the complexity of the TEDS conflict. Originally, we felt the protest was merely a matter of collective resistance to distasteful government regulations comparable to the truckers' strike or farmers protest of the 1970s. While there are striking similarities with these conflicts, there are also glaring differences.

The TEDS conflict is more of a Kafkaesque drama than most protests. The drama is not limited to a single dimension nor is its conclusion imminent. Discord wedded contention, and the natural resource dispute (turtles and shrimp) spawned dissension. The TEDs players argue about the laws and policies, about the moral character of the individuals and groups caught up in the dispute, about the words chosen to represent the problem, as well as the efficacy of TEDs. In short, the conflict is a bewildering collection of plots and subplots. We found issues embedded within other issues in a seemingly endless pattern of conflict.

Researching this tangle of plots challenged our abilities. We did not do our research in the rarefied air of a laboratory or in the quiet atmosphere of a library but amidst the clamor at public meetings and along the docks. Our general approach incorporated a random sample of Louisiana shrimpers augmented by a nonrandom sample of shrimpers from Texas, Florida, Georgia, and the Carolinas. We interviewed shrimpers in their homes or on the docks, whichever location was convenient for them. The survey included questions that ranged from personal opinion to employment history.

In addition, we examined a variety of documents, including letters, reports, minutes. We interviewed more than one hundred people who were either players in or close observers of the TEDs conflict. Included among these informants were shrimpers in leadership positions, fish shed owners, shrimp processors, government representatives, and environmentalists.

Our general approach was to present the "big picture." Rather than limit our examination to one or two tidy research questions, we chose to highlight the interconnections among different dimensions of the conflict. Accordingly, the drama is reconstructed from the accounts given by our informants. We tried to trace the events of the TEDs conflict as an unfolding story.

When the study was initiated at the end of 1989, many respondents made it clear that they expected us to uncover the truth. Of course, we have no single truth to report. It is neither possible nor advisable to judge which party is right and which is wrong. We have tried to track down and interview every player in the TEDs conflict within the limits of our time and resources. We listened to both sides of the controversy as well as those who counted themselves as neutrals. But the tug toward partisanship is strong even for the scientists who study conflicts, as the literature attests. Neutrality is at least partially an illusion.

During our investigation, we were conscious of the difficulties we faced safeguarding objectivity. Generally, we tried to follow the canons of science by holding up every fact and conclusion to the scrutiny of the principle of falsification.[2] We probed for the evidence that would falsify the opinion toward which we leaned. Wherever possible, we tried to garner independent evidence from a variety of sources (interviews, documents, direct observations, etc.) before drawing conclusions. Our goal was to separate the polemics appearing in the heat of conflict from verifiable fact. In attempting to disclose the objective truth, we became privy to the way parties try to construct reality, but we were also exposed to the seduction of taking sides. And we faced that perennial temptation that every researcher faces— namely, drawing conclusions prematurely. Of course, we tried to guard ourselves against substituting our personal opinions for the gaps in the facts. We trust the reader's judgment as to whether or not we have succeeded. But, in order to assess objectivity, one must consider the threats to it.

Objectivity is particularly threatened whenever there is a strong temptation to assume the role of player. Choosing sides is as much a problem for researchers as it is for parties to a conflict. Yet, compassion for shrimpers or environmental causes could turn research into sympathetic advocacy. Moreover, researchers sometimes have, as others do, stakes in the outcome of their research. We, after all, are interested in continued funding. Thus, researchers may be tempted to instrumental advocacy or seduced into becoming court scientists. In either case objectivity is compromised. But to pursue objectivity is not the same as achieving it, and scientists are no more inclined to be sinless than are all the other heirs of Adam.

In writing about TEDS, we relied more on the unstructured interviews and conversations with informants than on the structured survey of shrimpers. These "soft" methods of field research have a long and rich history in the social sciences.[3] It is an accepted conclusion of contemporary social scientists that both survey and field research are useful designs and that each strategy has a role to play in research that cannot be replaced by the other. We chose not to build our work primarily on the information we had gathered from our structured survey because these data tempted us to focus on the narrower concerns of fishery management problems. Above all else, we wanted to keep our promise to those who took the time to talk to us about TEDS. Our promise was to tell the whole story of TEDS to the best of our ability. We ardently hope that those who so graciously gave of their time and trusted us to faithfully record their accounts will find reason to believe that we have done so.

Introduction
THE CAST OF CHARACTERS

Shrimpers can be found in the southeast from Texas to North Carolina as well as on the northwest coast. However, since northwest shrimpers were not subject to the TEDs regulations, they were not included in the present study.

Although shrimpers share a common occupation to which they have an abiding personal attachment, shrimpers are a diverse group. Some own their vessels; others are hired captains in the employ of owners who may own a fleet of vessels. Some shrimp part-time and are called "weekend warriors" by full-time shrimpers. Some shrimpers target only shrimp, but some harvest fish and crabs as well. And the vessels from which they harvest the bounty of the sea are as diverse as the men and women who sail them. The sixteen-foot wooden or fiberglass vessels harvest the bays for a day or so at most before returning to port. By contrast, the steel-hulled vessels, over ninety feet and equipped with a freezer, venture offshore for weeks or even months at a time.

But whether they shrimp in small or large vessels or whether they pursue shrimp offshore or in shallow bays, shrimpers do not believe they endanger turtles. They simply do not believe that stranded turtle carcasses, whose presence on beaches coincide with shrimping seasons, can be attributed to them.

Shrimping, of course, is an industry involving buyers, processors, importers, exporters, wholesalers, and retailers. Obviously, not everyone in the industry shrimps for a living, but all are players in the TEDs drama and have stakes in the resource. Representing the larger vessel owners, the Texas Shrimp Association (TSA) played a significant role in the conflict. Government officials routinely assumed the TSA and the Louisiana Shrimp Association represented the industry, but the latter had far less influence in government circles than TSA. Both organizations were challenged in the 1980s by a grassroots movement that grew out of the concern among many shrimpers that those who shrimp for a living were not adequately represented. The Concerned Shrimpers of America was organized to respond to what many shrimpers felt was an increasingly hostile regulatory climate in general and to TEDs in particular. Through this organization, Louisiana shrimper Tee John Mialjevich drew members from all existing organizations and unified shrimpers from North Carolina to Texas in opposition to TEDs.

Typically, recreational harvesters present little competition to commercial harvesters. Recreational harvesters usually take shrimp, crab, and finfish by hook and line and small nets and traps. They do not sell their catch. However, it is not difficult to sell one's catch, despite laws that prohibit the practice and fines that are supposed to deter it. By the 1970s an increasing number of recreational or sportfishers with larger vessels and more sophisticated gear were challenging the primacy of commercial harvesters. Furthermore, recreational harvesters have organized and lobby state and federal legislatures regularly. In Louisiana, where every auto license plate declares the state to be the "sportsman's paradise," the Gulf Coast Conservation Association (GCCA) has effectively lobbied in Baton Rouge on behalf of their constituents.[1]

Those with an interest in the shrimping industry include, along with shrimpers, landowners who lease water rights to clubs and private individuals, manufacturers of fishing equipment, and sporting goods retail outlets and marinas. But a still wider circle can be drawn which has a financial stake in the leisure uses of coastal resources. Condos, hotels, recreational communities, and, more recently, gaming boats and barges are only some of the elements of a leisure industry that has an economic interest in the way marine resources are used.

Just as the shrimping industry included a variety of factions, so did the government entities that played various roles in the TEDs conflict. The National Marine Fisheries Service (NMFS), mandated to protect sea turtles, is responsible for designing and enforcing fishery regulations intended to sustain economic benefits to commercial fishers. Accordingly, NMFS designed the TED in the hopes that it would protect turtles and yet permit trawling, which was increasingly being assailed by environmentalists. The U.S. Fish and Wildlife Service (FWS), an agency of the Department of the Interior, is mandated to identify (list) and try to recover endangered or threatened species. Understandably, FWS aggressively pushed TEDs.

Created by the national Sea Grant College Program Act of 1966, the Sea Grant Extension Service, a sister agency with NMFS under the National Oceanic and Atmospheric Administration (NOAA) within the Department of Commerce, played an educational role.[2] Under the auspices of NOAA and the states in which they serve, marine agents of Sea Grant are expected to transfer fishery technology and inform commercial fishers on fishery regulations. Therefore, through newsletters and workshops, they spread the word on the TEDs regulations. But Sea Grant scientists also did scientific research that was subsequently used in the debate over TEDs. Scientists, both in Sea Grant and outside it, found it difficult to distance themselves from the conflict.

State governments also took action. The State of Florida implemented TEDs in state waters. Louisiana enacted anti-TEDS regulations and sued the U.S. government to block the enforcement of TEDS.

Environmentalists, chiefly the Center for Marine Conservation, with headquarters in Washington, D.C., coordinated the drive to protect sea turtles. Formerly called the Center for Environmental Education, the Center has worked on a variety of environmental issues including marine debris, fish conservation, and the Gulf shrimp fishery.[3] The Center and its staff and scientists are frequently sought after for advice and technical assistance in the formulation of fishery regulations. In short, it is a major player in marine policy development.

In its 1993 financial statement, the Center lists numerous foundations, some government agencies, corporations, and individuals as contributors.[4] Its critics argue that it depends on funding from large corporations, including corporations with poor environmental records. Although the Center coordinated the concern for sea turtles that had existed within the environmental community for at least twenty years, it did not reflect the attitudes of all environmentalists, particularly those who wished to distance themselves from "corporate polluters" and corporate donors.

The oil industry and the waste disposal industry are also key players in the TEDS conflict but for quite different reasons. The oil industry in the Gulf of Mexico, besides being a major client of waste disposal companies, has affected the environment through canal building. It has also facilitated shrimping by supplying locals with capital investment (better salaries) and flexible work schedules. The unintended consequence has been, particularly since the downturn in the oil industry, more shrimping effort and more part-timers in the fishery.

Historically, shrimpers have cooperated with environmental groups to fight pollution. But with so many players and so many interests being served, the debate surrounding the TEDS conflict could not be restricted to just shrimp versus turtles.

THE ISSUES

Contention over shrimp versus turtles spread to the efficacy of TEDS in particular and trawls in general. Opponents of trawls argue that they are indiscriminate and wasteful (the bycatch in shrimp trawls includes small unusable finfish).

Fishery regulations are also part of the contention. Since the enactment of the Magnuson Act in 1976,[5] the Department of Commerce has relied on the eight regional fishery councils for recommendations. In the area covered by the TEDS conflict, the Gulf of Mexico Fishery Management Council and the South Atlantic Fishery Management Council are relevant. The formula used to make appointments to these councils opens the door to political intrigue.[6] The councils are often split along commercial fishing versus recreational fishing lines. Often, too, a single vote decides whether a particular recommendation is made to the Secretary of the Department of Commerce. Partly as a result of the political nature of Councils, commercial harvesters find it difficult to separate other regulations from TEDS. In part, this misperception is understandable because the majority of Louisiana shrimpers land other species besides shrimp; clearly, they have economic reasons for having opinions about the management plans of other species. But the TEDS conflict kept alive other fishery conflicts because it seemed to commercial harvesters to be a pattern and plan of rich elites to rid the waters of commercial harvesters.

Commercial harvesters cite the example of redfish (red drum). This fish is highly favored by commercial fishers, recreational fishers, and restaurant clienteles. As a result of overfishing, government placed a moratorium on the commercial harvesting of redfish. Although some people believe that the popularization of a dish, blackened redfish, created by a local chef, gave rise to increased redfish fishing, thus greatly reducing the stock,[7] fishery scientists argue that the stock would have declined anyway. Even so, shrimpers, commercial fishers, and some government officials doubt the validity of these scientific predictions. Many shrimpers interpret the moratorium as an attempt by sportfishers to eliminate all commercial harvesters.

In 1990 government initiated a plan to reduce red snapper and other finfish incidentally caught and killed in shrimp trawls. Shrimpers believe that this action is also deliberately intended to hurt shrimpers. The TEDS issue, therefore, has become linked with other fishery regulations.

But the list of issues still does not stop here. The TEDS controversy unearthed embedded issues. Shrimpers believe that the TEDS regulations are payment for their past grassroots resistance to waste disposal plans in the Gulf.[8] Accordingly, Waste Management, they believe, has instigated, if not orchestrated, the effort by the national environmental community to save sea turtles. Shrimpers maintain that in Waste Management's effort to punish the shrimpers and distract attention away from pollution problems in the Gulf, the company has supplied both funds and legal services to the national environmental community.[9] Our present purpose is to forewarn the reader of the perplexing entanglement of issues.

Attempts to save endangered or threatened sea turtles from incidental taking by shrimpers caused unanticipated problems for all concerned.

*Caught
in the Net*

Chapter

1

Turtles and TEDS
THE HISTORY OF A CONFLICT

Sociologically, problems are both objective and subjective facts.[1] One can distinguish between, for example, poverty as the objective condition affecting people from society's awareness of and resolve to remedy the conditions of the poor. The misery of the poor was, in all likelihood, similar in the 1950s and the 1960s. The difference between the two decades was primarily that society waged war on poverty in the 1960s. In the 1960s America "discovered" poverty and developed a collective awareness of it as unconscionable. The scattered misery of many had been transformed into a singular sociological reality, the poor. Similarly, prior to the early 1970s, when environmentalists focused national attention on the plight of sea turtles, loss of hatcheries, egg poaching, pollution, and overharvesting of turtles had been commonplace for decades. But awareness of the turtle problem came to match the gravity of the objective problems only in the early 1970s.

THE TURTLE PROBLEM

As long as the plight of sea turtles was recognized only by scattered and unorganized individuals, very little could be done to reduce the threats to these species. What was necessary was organization and the mobilization of resources. Just as scattered clergy and social reformers could not have created the societal awareness of poverty, so, too, unorganized naturalists and scientists could not have engineered awareness of the turtle problem.

The ecology movement of the 1960s heightened social awareness of environmental issues and mobilized people and resources. By the early 1970s environmental organizations, well funded and bureaucratically organized, could successfully target a number of environmental problems. In the 1970s environmentalists began to pressure government to address the dangers facing marine sea turtles. With the passage of the Endangered Species Act (ESA) in 1973, a new and powerful instrument of protection was available. By the middle of the 1970s, a number of environmental organizations joined voices and called upon the Secretary of Commerce to protect threatened sea turtles. One of the causes of turtle mortality is the incidental taking of sea turtles in shrimp trawls. It is ironic that shrimpers supplied government scientists with information on turtle migration, beach strandings, as well as the number, type, and location of turtles caught in shrimp trawls. These data were ultimately used to estimate the impact of shrimping on turtle mortality.

The link between shrimping and turtle mortality rests on essentially two pieces of evidence, one direct and the other indirect. Turtles are caught in shrimp trawls. This is an incontestable fact. What is arguable is the number caught and the mortality rate. Captured turtles may be dead when taken aboard, or they may be stressed and drowning. Some are relatively unscathed by the experience. Distressed turtles can often be revived. The fact that in the past shrimpers would eat or sell the turtles they caught has strengthened the belief that shrimpers endanger sea turtles.

The indirect evidence linking shrimpers with turtle mortality is the correlation between shrimping effort and turtle strandings. Generally, sea turtle carcasses are found stranded on beaches during trawling peaks. Since turtle carcasses have been found in the absence of shrimping effort and their mortality, in some cases, can be attributed to other causes, shrimpers feel they are being singled out. They argue that beach development, poaching of turtle eggs, rig removal, and pollution have killed turtles. Yet, the government estimates that as many as fifty thousand turtles are incidentally taken in trawls each year.[2] The incidental taking of turtles is not the only problem the environmental community has with trawls.

Environmental and conservation groups have called attention to the wastefulness of trawls and the aesthetic degradation they cause to beaches. In addition to turtles, trawls incidentally take finfish, crabs, and other marine species, as well as marine debris. The bycatch, or at least some portion of it, is discarded. Trawls then are indiscriminate and, therefore, wasteful. Furthermore, small fish discarded by trawlers often wash up on beaches. Since the mid-1980s trawling has been blamed for depressing the stock of important commercial and recreational species. For these reasons, gear experts have been interested for some time in ways to modify trawls to make them more discriminating. It comes as no surprise, then, that those attempting to solve the problem associated with the incidental catch of turtles in trawls would consider technical solutions.

THE TECHNICAL SOLUTION

The National Marine Fisheries Service (NMFS) is charged with both protecting turtles and managing the fisheries that impact them. Under the guidelines of the Endangered Species Act, three solutions were available to NMFS.[3] First, NMFS could have elected to limit or shut down the fishery—clearly, a politically unacceptable solution. Second, it could have established an acceptable quota for incidental taking, much the way the porpoise quota was established for the tuna industry. Logistics and costs made this alternative prohibitive. Finally, the agency could have required the release of incidentally captured turtles. Obviously favored by the industry, this latter alternative was adopted and guidelines for resuscitating and releasing turtles were distributed. Contemporaneously, NMFS, Sea Grant Extension Service, and the shrimping industry embarked on a gear research effort. NMFS picked up the bill for the development of TEDS. According to one estimate, $3.4 million was spent on the TEDS development program.[4] However, in a personal interview in October of 1990, Chuck Oravetz, in charge of the Protected Species office within NMFS, disputed previously published claims of costs.[5] He argued that the total outlay was closer to $2 million. Whatever the costs incurred were, from the government's standpoint, a successful prototype emerged by 1980. It was the second of two designed strategies used.

Oravetz claimed that in 1978 "we spent several hundred thousand to develop a barrier device; these excluded about 75 percent of the turtles, and the shrimp loss was 15 to 30 percent."[6] The results were unacceptable, so a new strategy was used. Instead of keeping turtles from entering the trawl, a release device strategy was developed. Based on the principle already employed in devices used by shrimpers to exclude sea grass and other undesired organisms, the new strategy resulted in a technical success. In 1980 the first experiments with a TED were initiated. In the turtle-rich waters off eastern Florida, particularly the Cape Canaveral area, NMFS's TEDS were able to exclude 97 percent of the turtles entering the trawl. Based on these encouraging results, a voluntary program was initiated. The new device was an instant failure. Shrimpers complained that it was dangerous (the metal TED can hit an inattentive shrimper as the net is lifted on board), it lost shrimp, and it did not work. NMFS officials responded to these complaints. While the original purpose of a TED was to exclude turtles and maintain catch, subsequent modifications took other considerations into account. Fishery managers believed that from both a technical standpoint and a selling standpoint, overall bycatch reduction would be a welcomed addition to the redesigned TED. Furthermore, fishery managers believed that shrimpers that encounter turtles less frequently than Atlantic shrimpers needed more incentive to adopt TEDS. Thus, exclusion of turtles, maintenance of catch, and the exclusion of unwanted catch were all part of the design objectives. In 1983 a smaller, lighter, collapsible TED was introduced. It reduced daytime bycatch by 78 percent and nighttime bycatch by 50 percent. NMFS officials hoped that once shrimpers realized the device could save fuel costs through drag reduction—the less the bycatch, the less the drag—they would be eager to adopt it. In 1983 NMFS and the environmental community were convinced the new device worked, and a voluntary program was formally launched. NMFS distributed TEDS to shrimpers who agreed to use them. By volunteering, shrimpers could acquire a TED without paying the cost—two to three hundred dollars per TED. The agency spread the word through Sea Grant Extension newsletters, and marine agents demonstrated the new device at workshops conducted all along the coast. NMFS rebaptized the TED. It was promoted as a "Trawl Efficiency Device." Despite these ministrations, their hope for a voluntary adoption was not realized. Shrimpers for the most part remained skeptical and were not impressed by the new device.[7]

By 1985 the voluntary program was simply not working. Meanwhile, NMFS was getting pressure from the environmental community and the Fish and Wildlife Service (FWS), with whom NMFS shares the burden of protecting endangered and threatened species. Despite the money, time, and human resources expended, NMFS was frustrated in its attempts to satisfy both the requirements of the ESA and the wishes of the industry. While some commentators prefer to place the blame on NMFS, as some individuals connected with FWS, Sea Grant Extension Service, and the environmental community want to do, others argue that shrimpers have been both hard-headed and short-sighted in not adopting TEDS. Still others argue that both NMFS and the shrimpers are at fault. Charges and countercharges do nothing to clarify the issue, but some of the difficulty with the voluntary program can be traced to the nature of technical solutions and the diversity of the fishery.

THE TECHNICAL FIX

Technical solutions that require high levels of skill and/or motivation are inherently difficult to transfer. All knowledgeable parties and, most important, gear experts argue that for TEDS to work correctly they must be installed correctly and used correctly. It is not uncommon for rather small adjustments in the device to have major impacts on shrimp loss.[8] Gear experts themselves have admitted that they have occasionally improperly installed a TED which resulted in failure of the device.

Shrimpers in the South Atlantic had a higher adoption rate of TEDS than those in the Gulf. Some Sea Grant Extension Service officials believe that marine agents on the South Atlantic coast did a better job instructing shrimpers and accordingly experienced a higher rate of adoption, but our conversations with marine agents did not support this conclusion.[9] Since the marine agents appeared to us to be professional, highly motivated, and conscientious, we believe that the differences in the rate of TEDS adoptions are linked to the diversity of the fishery.

In fact, turtles are simply more abundant in some areas than in others. Clearly, a shrimper who rarely encounters a turtle is less likely than one who frequently does to graciously accept an encumbrance for which he sees no need. Although this is not the only factor affecting adoption rates, it makes clear that the failure of the voluntary program was not simply the result of the incompetence of a federal agency or the hard-headedness of shrimpers.

In summary, by 1983 NMFS's technical solution, based in part on devices already used by shrimpers to rid their trawls of unwanted bycatch and trash, was improved. Despite its technical success, it was an instant social failure. NMFS was unsuccessful in convincing the majority of shrimpers to voluntarily adopt TEDS. Throughout the voluntary period, a number of management decisions at all levels within the Department of Commerce were made to bring about a timely solution. The result of these collective decisions was conflict not only between the shrimping industry and the environmental community, but between these players and NMFS. Furthermore, the issue strained relations between federal agencies (NMFS and Sea Grant Extension) and between the state and the federal agencies involved.

MANAGEMENT DECISIONS AND INTERAGENCY CONFLICT

Decisions to pursue a technical solution to the turtle problem set into motion a cooperative effort between NMFS and Sea Grant Extension Service that eventually led to conflict between the two agencies and the isolation of NMFS during the mandatory phase of TEDS.

As will be explored later in greater detail, in the early 1970s major reshuffling of agencies' roles occurred. Sea Grant Extension Service, modeled after the Agricultural Extension Service, assumed some of the roles NMFS previously played, most notably the educational and service mission. The Magnuson Act of 1976 mandated NMFS to play a regulatory role. In effect, it was called upon to play the "bad guy" without previously having the opportunity to play the "good guy" through direct service to the industries it regulated. By contrast, Sea Grant Extension Service established its marine agents in coastal communities and earned a good record of delivering educational services to its constituents. Although state Sea Grant Extension Service structures vary somewhat among coastal states, marine agents generally become trusted friends to commercial fishers and accepted members in the communities in which they work.

The division of labor between NMFS and Sea Grant Extension Service worked reasonably well prior to the emergence of unpopular regulations, although, according to officials of both agencies, some friction existed when NMFS had to give up its service role.[10] It was in this interagency context that the voluntary program was launched.

By 1985 the environmental community was pressing NMFS to make TEDS mandatory. Other voices, such as FWS, the agency that was responsible for the majority of listings under the ESA, were also raised against NMFS's failure to get shrimpers to adopt TEDS. By the time the Center for Marine Conservation wrote the Secretary of Commerce informing him of their intention to sue under the provisions of the ESA, NMFS officials felt abandoned. Their successful technical solution to the turtle problem, TEDS, had alienated them from the shrimping industry. Their desire to minimize the negative impacts of the ESA was seen by the environmental community as foot-dragging and timidity. Their enthusiasm to get marine agents to convince shrimpers to adopt TEDS succeeded in alienating some Sea Grant people. As one high ranking NMFS official complained: "We were alone. We had to take all the blame."[11]

With the obvious failure of the voluntary program and the continuing evidence of turtle strandings, the environmental community began to apply increasing pressure on the Department of Commerce to abide by the law of the land, the Endangered Species Act. Eventually mediation gave way to new political and legal battles.

In early 1986 the regional director of Fish and Wildlife Service (FWS) in Atlanta joined with turtle advocates and appealed to the Gulf Fishery and Management Council to require TEDS on all shrimp trawls.[12] Under the Magnuson Act, the Council was mandated to develop plans to manage fisheries. The Council had played no direct role in the development of TEDS. Furthermore, the Council develops and recommends fishery plans, but it is ultimately up to the Department of Commerce to adopt or not adopt recommended plans. The Shrimp Committee of the South Atlantic Council did recommend the mandatory use of TEDS on shrimp vessels at times and places determined by sea turtle concentrations. These recommendations were incorporated into the first set of regulations created at the southeast regional office of NMFS. In the fall of 1986, NOAA called a meeting and briefed environmentalists and the industry on the proposed regulations. Having been informed by the Center for Marine Conservation of its intent to sue NMFS under the provisions of ESA, NOAA was hoping these regulations would avert a legal battle. The proposed regulations, however, were unacceptable to both environmentalists and the shrimping industry. Within days, the Center for Marine Conservation, joined by other national environmental organizations, served notice of their intention to sue and warned that if NMFS did not comply with the ESA provisions within sixty days, the suit would demand a closure of the shrimp fishery in all U.S. waters except those outside the range of sea turtles.

Faced with a closure, the Texas Shrimp Association requested mediation. In pursuing this path, NMFS and NOAA were turning new ground. While other federal agencies used negotiated rule-making with some success, it had not been used before by NMFS.

Hopes were high that the mediation meetings would produce an agreement. But Tee John Mialjevich, president of Concerned Shrimpers of America, refused to sign. TSA first accepted the agreement, then repudiated it. Shortly after the last negotiation session in December of 1986, the regulations mandating TEDS were published in the *Federal Register*.[13] An intense political and legal battle followed.

"IT'S NOT OVER 'TIL IT'S OVER"

From 1987 to 1989, TEDS regulations consumed the energies of an extraordinarily large number of people—the national environmental community, the shrimp industry, government agencies at the state and federal levels, Congress, the courts, and the White House.

Shrimpers, particularly in the Gulf and especially Louisiana, enjoyed considerable political support for their cause. In committees (for example, Merchant Marine and Fisheries headed by Congressman William Tausin of Louisiana) and on the floor of Congress, sympathetic legislators held up the ESA reauthorization and added amendments that required the National Academy of Science to investigate the turtle problem. The Office of Management and Budget (OMB) mandated that the technical and economic impacts of TEDS be studied. Shrimpers hoped that these studies would vindicate them. Throughout this period, shrimpers anxiously awaited the proof that would put an end to TEDS, but they did not relax their resistance to TEDS on other fronts.

Louisiana shrimpers successfully mobilized their supporters among their communities and elected and appointed officials. The Louisiana legislature quickly enacted laws that made the enforcement of TEDS requirements in state waters illegal. The Attorney General filed suit in the federal district court arguing that TEDS were unfair and that shrimpers were being denied due process. At the same time, however, Florida was passing TEDS regulations for its state waters.

In Louisiana shrimpers were successful in postponing TEDS. Amendments to the ESA delayed imposition of TEDS until 1989 offshore and 1990 in inshore waters. By 1988, however, it was clear that the courts would offer no hope for a cancellation or a longer postponement. The federal district court upheld the regulations. The case met a similar fate in the Fifth Circuit Court of Appeals. Furthermore, the shrimpers experienced no relief from TEDS from two studies that were prompted by their political resistance to TEDS. As the summer of 1989 approached, the long-awaited National Academy of Science (NAS) study on turtle mortality had not appeared. Neither had the TEDS Observer Program study mandated by OMB. The NAS study was published in 1990 after some delay and supported the government's position that shrimping was responsible for killing as many as fifty thousand turtles each year. But it also cast considerable doubt over the government's contention that there was no shrimp loss with TEDS.

The TEDS Observer Program, reporting on the technical aspects of the TEDS' effectiveness, was published in 1990 and noted some shrimp loss even with fine-tuned TEDS. Privately, some NMFS officials at Saint Petersburg and at Galveston, where the study was conducted, complained that shrimpers purposely made the TED-installed net lose shrimp.[14] The OMB-mandated study on the economic impact of TEDS languished even longer than the two aforementioned studies. The focus of the TEDS controversy had shifted from arguing about regulations and studies to securing delays in the imposition of and resistance to TEDS.

In the summer of 1989, many shrimpers in the central Gulf did not own a TED or know how to use one. Secretary David Mosbacher lifted the TEDS regulations to allow shrimpers time to comply. As the period of reprieve drew to an end, shrimpers complained of the unusual abundance of grass in the Gulf. Another postponement was granted while an assessment of the grass problem was made. When it was determined that the problem was not serious enough to warrant further delays, Mosbacher was still inclined to lift the regulations. However, the national environmental community secured a court order and TEDS were reimposed on July 21, 1989. The ordinarily hot summer on the Gulf coast became hotter.

A day before the on-again, off-again TEDS were to be reimposed, the president of Concerned Shrimpers promised a blockade of Gulf ports and waterways. Tee John Mialjevich warned that two thousand vessels would blockade Gulf ports.[15] The following day, hundreds of shrimp vessels did in fact block ports and shipping channels at Aransas, Corpus Christi, and Galveston, Texas, and at Cameron and Grand Isle (Belle Pass), Louisiana. For thirty-six hours the blockade paralyzed shipping. Emotions were running high and the talk of violence reverberated through the airways over shrimpers' radios. The shrimpers were determined to hold their positions, and the Coast Guard, whose responsibility it is to keep navigation channels open, was equally determined to clear the waterways. It was a standoff. Shrimpers demanded to speak with Mosbacher as the condition to ending the blockade. Unable to meet personally with shrimpers, Mosbacher sent three NOAA officials. Early Sunday morning on July 23, just thirty-six hours after it began, the blockade ended. Mialjevich persuaded the shrimpers to call it off. They would listen to no one else. The shrimpers awaited the decision of the Secretary of Commerce.

Mosbacher appears to have been sympathetic to the cause of shrimpers. Citing the high probability of violence, Mosbacher lifted the regulation. Immediately, the National Wildlife Federation and the Center for Marine Conservation filed

A unidentified shrimper holds a mangled grid, a product of the collision between trash and the TED. *Both natural (dense growth of sea grass) and human-made objects (oil pipeline debris and pilings) cause shrimp loss and render the* TED *ineffective. Abandoned pipelines and pilings ruin both net and* TED.

suit. The District Judge mandated turtle protection, but did not require the Secretary to reimpose TEDS. Under the temporary rules, Mosbacher gave shrimpers the option of either pulling TEDS or restricting tow times to 105 minutes (the assumption was that turtles could survive short tow times). This decision was unsatisfactory to the National Wildlife Federation (NWF). Arguing that only TEDS would adequately protect turtles, NWF challenged the Department of Commerce's tow-time compromise. In August of 1989, NWF went back to the Texas District Court to argue the need for TEDS. The shrimpers' hopes to be free of TEDS took still another roller coaster ride down. Despite Secretary Mosbacher's clear preference for some alternative to TEDS (e.g., tow-time limitations), by September of 1989 the reimposition of TEDS was inevitable. In what appeared in hindsight to be one last desperate attempt to resist, shrimpers blockaded Belle Pass near Grand Isle, while others greeted the visiting President George Bush at Belle Chasse, Louisiana, with TEDS protest signs. Despite presidential promises to look into the issue, shrimpers (at least, offshore shrimpers) had to either pull TEDS or evade enforcement. Many chose the latter. For the remainder of the 1989 shrimping season, compliance was low. At best, 40–50 percent of vessels boarded in the Central Gulf by the Coast

Guard were pulling a certified TED. Many shrimpers did not have a TED on board. Still others rendered them useless. Despite government's contention that compliance in 1989 was over 90 percent, both shrimpers and environmentalists knew better.

The 1990 season saw little improvement in the acceptance of TEDS by shrimpers. From Alabama to Texas, compliance remained unsatisfactory in the Central Gulf. By July, 1990, despite aggressive enforcement of civil penalties ($8,000 fines), many shrimpers felt they simply could refuse to pay the fines. In the words of Andy Kemmerer of NMFS, "We had to go criminal." Beginning in July of 1990, TEDS violations were prosecuted under criminal statutes. From 1991 to the present, resistance to and noncompliance with TEDS regulations has probably decreased. Turtle strandings are still common, and NMFS officials still maintain shrimpers are responsible. As recently as spring, 1995, NMFS threatened shrimpers with tougher regulations, including bans on shrimping in areas experiencing high turtle mortality.

Twenty years have passed since environmentalists first attempted to save sea turtles, and a decade has been spent promoting and mandating TEDS. It appears that both shrimpers and turtles are languishing.

To understand what went wrong, one must understand how the various components of the conflict contributed to the problem. The shrimpers' protest, governments' actions, the inability of science to settle scientific disputes, the environmental movement's challenge, the growth of a sportfishing lobby, and the discrepancies among various conservation laws all combined to make the TEDS conflict a contentious and protracted affair.

Although each component of the conflict played a unique role at different, but sometimes overlapping, time periods, the result was the same. The contending parties committed themselves to words and actions that made a reasonable compromise remote.

CAPTIVES OF CONFLICT

What happened in the TEDS case is that the stakeholders in the resource issue became, in time, dependent on the conflict; they became captives of conflict.[16] Our notion of the captivity process includes partisanship, but also other dimensions that can help us make sense of the perplexing and enduring TEDS drama.

Drawing upon our interviews from informants and documentary data, we have identified four generalizations about the captivity process: (1) captives of conflict have limited freedom; (2) as the conflict assumes a more important role, the resource issue is eclipsed; (3) captives have a stake in the conflict; and (4) the actions and reactions of captives become progressively divorced from reasonableness.

1. **Captivity.** The word *captive* denotes one who is not free. In the TEDS conflict, players limited their options once they became committed to the conflict. Time, energy, and resources are invested in the conflict and combatants lose some of their freedom to explore other options, including working towards a real compromise. The shrimper who spends his energy fighting TEDS, instead of shrimping, is a captive of the conflict. So too is the environmentalist whose zeal for TEDS has deflected attention away from other factors contributing to the problem, such as pollution. Similarly, other parties to the conflict become captives to the extent that the conflict restricted their freedom.

2. **Loss of resource issue.** Very early in the history of the conflict, the issue of turtles became eclipsed by the issues the conflict itself spawned. Combatants questioned the efficacy of TEDS, the legitimacy of the scientific facts, and each other's motives. Name calling and impugning each other's motives intensified the environment of mistrust. The issue of turtles was upstaged by the drama of the conflict. But despite the emotional claims and counterclaims, combatants did bring their vested interests to the arena of conflict. Furthermore, combatants not only developed stakes in the resource but in the conflict as well.

3. **Stakeholders.** Players are stakeholders to the extent to which they (*a*) derive a benefit from the conflict, (*b*) see their goals as being incompatible with the goals of other players, and (*c*) derive a sense of group unity from the differences over the conflict issues.[17] In brief, conflict is functional for stakeholders.

It is clear that it is in the interest of shrimpers to catch shrimp, not lose them. It logically follows that if they believe TEDS lose shrimp and that shrimping does not harm turtles, they will see no purpose in pulling TEDS. What is not so obvious is that shrimpers have a stake in perpetuating the conflict. This is so not only because it is their best hope of redressing an unfair regulation (from their point of view), but because conflict has become functional. It has unified them. It has given them organizational effectiveness and respect. Having drawn so many battle lines with so many foes—environmentalists, recreationists, and federal agencies— shrimpers have become captives of the conflict. As long as they benefit from the conflict, they will be tempted to perpetuate it. But as stakeholders and captives, shrimpers are not alone.

Besides having an abiding interest in saving turtles, environmentalists also have a stake in the conflict. Winning (as long as TEDS are mandatory, it is a win) a hard fight against a powerful foe enhances the environmental organizations' chances for continued funding, heightens commitment of rank-and-file members, and helps attract new members and funding sources. Indeed, a protracted confrontation with shrimpers is more rewarding for environmental groups than a decisive win. Once the threat to turtles is over or nearly so, members would begin to lose interest and funding would drop off. Theoretically, the most successful organization is one that gets ever closer to its goal but never completely achieves it.[18] But continued conflict with shrimpers is in the interest of environmentalists for still another reason.

Since some turtle experts have argued that the main cause of turtle mortality is not trawling, it is possible that full compliance with TEDS would not prevent continued decline or even a more rapid decline of turtle populations. A particularly difficult dilemma would result if necropsies initiated in 1991 reveal that pollution is a serious threat to turtle survival. In that event, environmentalists might face the oil and chemical companies as enemy, some of whom have contributed to the fight for TEDS. Under these conditions, it would be in the interest of environmental groups to continue the conflict with shrimpers. It is obviously possible for the turtle populations to rebound as a result of TEDS use. In this case, although further interest in turtles might wane, the success here could be parlayed into support to recover other endangered species. There is a danger, however, in claiming a temporal fluctuation as a success, when populations may resume a decline. Therefore, environmentalists have some stakes in an enduring conflict.

Recreationists also benefit from the conflict. The TEDS conflict has helped recreationists sustain the image of the shrimper as crude and hotheaded, an image that can sway public opinion. Recreationists contend that the use of trawls is an indiscriminate method of harvesting as shrimp trawls can incidentally take juvenile fish as well as turtles. Since 1990 shrimpers and other commercial harvesters have successfully fought off attempts to restrict trawling; however, many observers believe that shrimpers will ultimately be mandated to pull fish excluder devices, or as the government calls them, bycatch reduction devices.

TEDS have also drawn attention to bycatch, the abiding concern among recreational fishers. Adding to the bycatch controversy, many shrimpers supplement their income from shrimping by targeting red drum and speckle trout, species recreationists would like classified as game fish. Thus, recreational and commercial harvesters are in direct competition.

If the popular belief among shrimpers that the sportfishing lobby would like to rid the Gulf of all commercial harvesters is true, then a continuing TEDS conflict is in their interest.

The interest of federal agencies in the TEDS conflict contrasts sharply with the narrower objective of the recreational community. From the beginning of this controversy, many NMFS officials were unconvinced by the environmentalists' argument that other efforts, rather than just teaching shrimpers to revive turtles, were necessary. Thus, NMFS was reluctantly drawn into the conflict. Of course, the agency benefited from the funding allocated to deal with the problem and ultimately resulted in the development of TEDS. But the agency did not foresee how strongly shrimpers would resist voluntary adoption and how far environmentalists would go to stop the incidental taking of turtles. NMFS did not foresee that TEDS would be imposed in the entire Gulf and the South Atlantic, not just in turtle-rich waters. But once TEDS were developed, the conflict enveloped the agency. And the more intense the conflict became, the more NMFS tried to convince shrimpers and other parties to the conflict that TEDS worked. NMFS took the hard-sell stance, while its sister agency, Sea Grant Marine Extension Service, took the non-sell stance. Sea Grant did so partly because it was following its mandated nonadvocacy directive, but also because this position kept alive a long-standing tension between the two agencies. The discord was nothing extraordinary as far as interagency conflicts go, but it became intertwined with the TEDS conflict. Each agency derived from the conflict a sense of unity based on the differences (vis-à-vis TEDS) between them. Furthermore, each agency derived a sense of its unique mission from the experiences with TEDS, and this revived sense of mission increased the solidarity of the respective agencies.

The states of the Gulf and South Atlantic were able to use the TEDS conflict for economic and political gain. In Florida commercial harvesters have been routed by recreational interests. It is consistent with that state's interests to support the federal mandate, and, indeed, Florida subsequently imposed stricter state TEDS regulations. It is in the interest of the state to continue its policy of restricting commercial harvesters. By contrast, in Louisiana, commercial harvesters are an important economic and political sector, and recreational interests have only recently begun to mobilize their constituents. Understandably, Louisiana fought TEDS vigorously. Conflict is also functional for the state because it has old scores to settle with the federal government—namely, that officials in Washington, D.C. have accused Louisiana of having more than its share of corrupt politicians.

Louisiana's governor Edwin Edwards, no stranger to state and federal disputes, mobilized state agencies to fight TEDS. The legislature enacted anti-TEDS laws which blocked the enforcement of TEDS in state waters. And Louisiana's Attorney General William Guste filed suit in the federal district court to block TEDS. Louisiana could not countenance a major threat to its shrimping industry, particularly at a time when its oil revenues were plummeting. Moreover, politicians could use the TEDS conflict for political gain. Appointed officials of state agencies could also use the TEDS conflict to enhance the power and influence of the agencies, not to mention justify higher budget requests. Thus, state government also had a stake in the conflict.

Indeed, scientists have come to have a stake in the conflict. This is so not only because scientists are tempted to choose sides and become partisans, but because scientists stand to gain from the conflict.[19] Specifically, as the TEDS conflict heated up, more funds were made available to study both the biological and the social components of the TEDS conflict.

4. Loss of Reasonableness. Conflict, like other elementary social processes, is neither wholly rational nor wholly irrational. However, anyone who has witnessed a domestic argument knows that parties to an argument become preoccupied with the most charged elements in the controversy. They are no longer open to new experiences or interpretations. Actions and words lose reasonableness. In the TEDS case, the same level of turtle protection could be achieved with less hardships on shrimpers if the combatants could be steered off the collision course. Privately, many of the government officials and scientists we interviewed suggested that full compliance with TEDS in turtle-rich waters alone would have been as effective as the original regulations, and, they hasten to add, it would have been a more reasonable solution. At least initially, environmentalists were willing to "focus on areas we all agreed would be hot spots."[20] But in the heat of battle, combatants lose sight of their original goals. Subsequent actions are directed more toward the ongoing conflict than the resource issue which fathered it.

Thus, the captivity process contributed to the TEDS drama.

Chapter

2

Setting the Stage for Oil and Shrimp

To understand the continuing debate over TEDS regulations, we must first examine the forces that have altered life in coastal fishing communities and commercial harvesting.

Traditional coastal communities in America have had to adapt to two significant transformations—coastal development and offshore oil development. Both have altered the landscape and the lives of coastal inhabitants. Land development has been widespread along America's coasts. Following the residential preferences and leisure activities of Americans, it has had a greater impact in coastal areas with marketable amenities. Offshore oil exploration and development, however, has affected the coastal communities in Texas and Louisiana. The coastal changes in Louisiana have been largely a byproduct of offshore oil. Texas' coast has been changed both by offshore oil development and the growth of a leisure industry, reflecting the state's coastal amenities and availability of capital. Florida's changed coastline is more clearly a product of the influx of migrants and the expansion of the leisure industry. The remaining shrimp-producing states in the Southeast parallel Florida's development, although with much less intensity. Coastal development through the activities of a leisure industry are examined in chapter seven.

The great majority of southeast shrimpers are found in Texas and Louisiana (see fig. 1). Offshore oil in the central Gulf unleashed forces that changed both shrimping and shrimpers' life-styles. By modifying the traditional bases for work

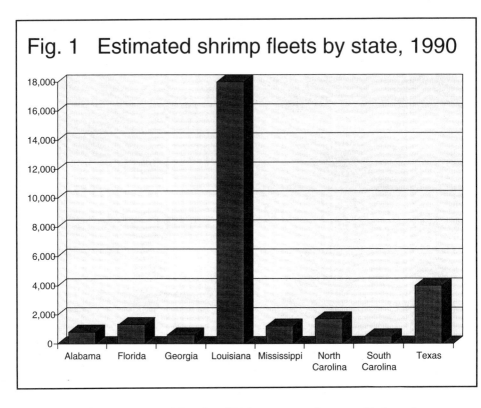

Fig. 1   Estimated shrimp fleets by state, 1990

in coastal fishing communities, the oil industry upset the natural balance between human beings and nature by encouraging the exploitation of marine resources and redefining the nature of work and leisure.

Shrimping and the offshore oil drilling are distinctly different types of economic activities. In a sense, they represent the old and the new. Significantly, they sustain two different types of social arrangements.[1] Conflict between these two industries is not unique or new.[2] Its origin is as old as the beginning of the Industrial Revolution and the end of feudalism. It is the perennial conflict between traditional and modern man.[3] The transformation that started in feudal Europe spread throughout the world. The traditional ways of living are inevitably altered by the modern industrial spirit. All over the globe, industrial development has transformed village life. Similarly, with the advent of oil and gas exploration in coastal Louisiana and Texas, fishing and farming villages were no longer protected from modern changes.

When modern America made its debut on the central Gulf coast, it brought with it immediate changes. But few worried about the the accompanying environmental costs or the new life-styles. The spirit of material progress soon changed the way people made their living.

FISHING AND OIL: CONTRASTING ECONOMIES

Fishing and oil industries compete for the same space and in many cases the same labor. Most shrimpers, indeed most fishers, are not wage workers. They either own or co-own vessels or work for shares of the catch. They work on vessels and follow flexible work schedules. Those who shrimp and fish exercise substantial freedom over their labor and time. Their occupational and familial lives are interwoven. Fishers are self-reliant and have a sense of adventure that is satisfied by encounters with the sea.[4] Fishing is organized around a renewable resource and uses mostly local capital. It provides an enduring and relatively constant way of life and a stable, but low, economic foundation, unless changes to the environment and/or the fishery occur. The oil industry is markedly different.

Drilling for offshore oil involves the movement of large amounts of capital typically from outside the extraction area. It necessitates wage labor and very precise schedules. The world of the offshore oil rig is both physically and psychologically separated from family life. Indeed the spheres of work and family may become sequestered.[5] Unlike fisheries, the offshore industry does not provide an enduring and constant economic base, but rather booms, busts, and uncertainties. More importantly, offshore development is, as is true of technology in general, a major agent of social change. It is the vehicle whereby the modern world breaches the walls that surround the parochial village. It ultimately changes the world it penetrates by first compromising with the subsistence economies that it encounters.[6]

The forces of change attendant to the introduction of oil had an enormous impact on shrimping in Texas and Louisiana. But nowhere has this impact been greater than in Acadia. The Cajun shrimper is at the center then of the encounter between shrimp and oil, between the old and the new.

THE TRADITIONAL CULTURE OF ACADIA

Historically, Cajuns have hunted, trapped, fished, and tended to dominate shrimping in Louisiana. They have also significantly influenced shrimping in other areas, particularly Texas.[7] To be sure, other groups have been affected, but the traditional culture of Acadia located along the coast of Louisiana was the most affected by the growth in the offshore oil industry. This culture would never be the same, but neither would it be erased, as shrimping, a core component, became locked into a symbiotic relationship, of accommodation and conflict, with the advancing rationality of offshore oil.

Commercial harvesting of marine resources, trapping, and farming have been the mainstay of the area's dominant ethnic group, the Cajun French. Even after oil and gas fields were discovered, the coastal populations of Louisiana managed to live symbiotically with the oil and gas industries. Employment in the oil and gas fields provided money to purchase larger vessels and gear or to improve existing vessels. For numerous Louisianians, employment in the oil and gas industry is what they have to do; fishing, shrimping, and trapping is what they want to do.

Much has been written about the traditional culture of South Louisiana, referred to as either Cajun culture or culture of Acadia.[8] Before the drilling for oil offshore, which began nearly half a century ago, the patterns of life were largely traditional. In order to understand the effects of offshore oil on shrimping, it is necessary to know something of the history and culture of Cajuns.

The majority of the people who reside in south Louisiana can trace their ancestry to the French settlers who were deported from Nova Scotia between 1755 and 1760.[9] The history of these people after they settled in rural Louisiana is not easy to follow; however, the vitality and assimilating effects of their culture are discernible. In the nineteenth century, an observer described the white coastal population of Louisiana as an "extremely heterogeneous ethnic mass".[10] Quickly, Anglo Americans and Europeans from Germany, France, Spain, Italy, and elsewhere were absorbed into the predominantly Acadian culture of south Louisiana.[11] It is bewildering to visitors to Acadia to be introduced to Cajuns named Waguespack, Schexnayder, and a host of other names with a greater affinity with Germany and southeastern Europe than France. Yet, the homogeneity of the culture often obscures the diverse origins of the people who embody it.

> [Acadians] are a homogeneous people of French descent set apart from neighboring groups by language, religion, and customs, and have maintained in unaltered simplicity many of the ways and manners of their forefathers. While holding tenaciously to the lands settled by their progenitors, these people have resolutely resisted cultural influences which have been impinging upon them from surrounding groups. Indeed, they have shown an unlimited capacity for absorbing the extraneous population elements coming among them. In many cases they have stamped the offspring of intermarriages with their own customs and traditions, the change from Anglo Saxon to a French cultural heritage sometimes taking place in a single generation. The degree to which members of this group have retained old forms and customs and the success they have had in repelling influences from other population groups make them a particularly significant group to study.[12]

The mass of Acadians belonged to the poorer classes. They should not be confused with Creole planters, those wealthy and sometimes more worldly bon vivants. The ancestors of Cajuns were rural folk of France before settlement in Nova Scotia and resettlement in Louisiana. These facts figure importantly on their present occupational patterns and status. To these poorer peoples, the swamps and rivers of south Louisiana furnished economic opportunities not available to poorer classes in other areas.

> The bayous contained an unlimited supply of fish which could be caught either for consumption or for market. The forests and marsh lands afforded an abundant animal life which could be trapped or hunted for food or for fur. Then, there were certain valuable woods which grew in the swamps and could be hunted out and marketed. In addition, vegetables grew prolifically the year round, and the family could raise much of its food on a small garden plot. To this list must be added Spanish moss which grows profusely in the forests and has long been gathered for market. Fishing, hunting, trapping, and the gathering of moss and woods, in addition to the growing of vegetables, therefore, helped to make the swamps a favorable retreat for the whites who were not included in the plantation system.[13]

Being self-employed in one or all of these pursuits allows Cajuns to set their own work schedules. They can work when they want to or when they need to. For a Cajun the business of life is not business; it is living. Cajuns genuinely enjoy these activities and the family life these pursuits sustain. Cajun shrimpers that we interviewed spoke of the good life, something to be enjoyed. Although they sometimes expressed anger and frustration over what their lives have become, they never spoke of it as boring. Very often, they connected shrimping with freedom—not the freedom of contemporary American individualism but the freedom to be with family. In their spare time they "hunt, fish, trap, and spend time with family." They enjoy catching, cooking, and eating the bounty nature has so richly supplied them. And the enjoyment is doubled because it is shared by kin. This is the core of Cajun culture.[14]

The idea that humans do not naturally and continually seek to increase their standard of living may seem foreign to contemporary America. To be guided by values outside the marketplace is, of course, what traditionalism means. To preeminently seek and rationally pursue economic increase must be learned, for without such teaching people maintain their parochial outlook. The single most important impediment to the development of capitalism is the constellation of values that one finds in traditionalism.[15] This idea is critical to understanding how the introduction of offshore oil has changed shrimping. The spirit of modernism came to the central Gulf with the arrival of offshore oil. This spirit unintentionally teaches that almost everything, including traditional ways, can be evaluated in economic terms. The coming of offshore hastened the modernization of the central Gulf.

AN INTRUSION OF RATIONALITY: OIL WORK

The drilling for offshore oil represents the greatest intrusion to the traditional culture of Acadia. Oil ushered in the modern spirit that challenges traditions and threatens to replace them with more rational monetary ones. It embellished the need for getting ahead and credit buying. It also brought with it a unique work schedule for a modern society accustomed with its weekly and diurnal cycles.

The exploration for and extraction of deposits of oil and gas principally occur in remote, inaccessible areas under coastal waters. Transportation between these offshore worksites and onshore support bases requires considerable expense and extensive time. In order to reduce this expense, altered work schedules have developed.[16]

The typical pattern for offshore work is for employees to meet at a designated site in order to be transported offshore by either helicopter or boat. A worker will normally stay offshore for 7 days, but stays of 14, 21, or 28 are not unusual. Following the offshore stay, the employee is returned to the meeting site and has a period of days off, typically the same length as the stay offshore, although some variations occur in these patterns (e.g., fourteen days on with seven days off). These patterns of offshore employment have continued for over four decades.[17] An individual who works this concentrated work schedule is typically away from his family for extended periods of time and then home for extended periods. Appropriately, this has been called a feast-or-famine schedule.[18] But the undesirability of this work schedule is relative. To some shrimpers or fishers, it actually means more time at home than harvesting offshore. Although little research has been conducted on the adaptations of the families of offshore oil workers, existing research written suggests that offshore oil workers make the same kind of adaptations as fishers.[19] Essentially, they also face the same problems. However, except for local oil workers who work on foreign coasts, work schedules of oil workers give them more time to be with their families than offshore shrimpers.

Along with the gradual increase in the drilling for offshore oil came, of course, an increase in demand for offshore oil workers. But the demand for offshore oil workers was always such that workers were able to quit anytime they wished to shrimp or fish and just as easily resume oil work whenever they wished. For many offshore oil workers shrimping and fishing have become a recreational and economic pastime. In a recent study of 161 families of offshore oil workers, 70 percent had a boat that was used for shrimping.[20]

Shrimping and offshore oil work share a close relationship. Offshore oil workers often quit during shrimping season to devote full time to the occupation they enjoy. They return to oil work when they need to. This shift between shrimping and oil has allowed the culture to survive. One shrimper commented on this work pattern: "During the good times we would take off during shrimp season. We would miss about three hitches which means about six weeks. You didn't have to worry about your oil field job because they needed so many people you could always get a job."[21] Another shrimper expressed similar opinions: "The only things I like about working offshore are the money and the time off. When I am off I shrimp, trap, hunt, or whatever season it is. Working offshore lets me do the things I really want to do. Man, I would love to shrimp and trap for a living. But I got a family, bills; there is just no way I could make it. If it were not for this offshore job I probably wouldn't shrimp at all. I would sell my boat if I didn't work offshore."[22]

The 1980s brought a decline in oil field work, and the supply of workers vastly outnumbered the demand; consequently, the freedom to quit also disappeared. But the 1990s brought an increase in overseas drilling, and more workers were put on extended on-off day schedules (28 days on with 28 days off, or 60 days on with 60 days off).

Offshore work schedules remain culturally attractive to some shrimpers because of the recurring on-off cycle. It still allows workers to shrimp, fish, and trap, although not with as much freedom as before. An offshore oil worker commented about how the reduced number of oil field jobs affected his shrimping activities: "You cannot quit a job and find another so easy. Things have changed. . . . It has affected the time I can shrimp and trap. Use to be the offshore job revolved around my shrimping. Now my shrimping revolves around my offshore job. I am afraid they are going to ask me to go foreign; that means a 60-60 schedule. I don't know how that would affect my shrimping time. You could possibly miss a whole season."[23]

For many offshore oil workers, shrimping is now a pastime. Commenting on the change, a Louisiana shrimper claimed: "Every kid has been shrimping. Everybody around here knows how to shrimp. Shrimping is our pastime. If you got some spare time, you get an ice chest full of ice, some beer, and gas, and you go shrimping."[24]

IMPACT OF OFFSHORE OIL
ON SHRIMPING AND SHRIMPERS

Historically, the United States shrimp fishery of the Gulf and South Atlantic, was largely confined to white shrimp, *Penaeus setiferus*.[25] Shrimp were taken by traditional methods and vessels were relatively small. The economic life of many Gulf and South Atlantic coastal communities was tied exclusively to the shrimp fishery and other forms of harvesting.

After World War II and the development of offshore oil, shrimping in the Gulf changed. The Tortugas shrimp fishery off the south Florida coast and the brown shrimp fishery off the Texas and Louisiana coasts have rapidly developed.[26] The pink shrimp, *Penaeus duorarum,* concentrated off south Florida and the more important brown shrimp, *Penaeus aztecus,* concentrated off Texas' and Louisiana's coastlines, were targeted by shrimpers willing to venture in the deeper waters for longer intervals. The nocturnal browns and pinks are pursued with larger vessels and more sophisticated gear and electronic equipment. More and larger vessels entered the fishery, and shrimp production increased markedly.

Although the line is not always sharply drawn, offshore shrimping and inshore shrimping require different strategies. In the Gulf offshore shrimpers primarily target larger shrimp. Browns and whites, *Penaeus aztecus* and *P. setiferus,* respectively, are the most important. Pinks and several other species are also taken but are under 10 percent of the total catch. Many offshore shrimpers, regardless of their home port, make the run from the Tortugas off south Florida to Texas. Although one week in and one week out is the typical shrimping rhythm, shrimpers in the offshore fishery may be away from their home port for weeks or months at a time. Cajun shrimpers were the first to travel farther afield to pursue large shrimp in the deeper waters. According to one shrimper, "I made it in shrimping because I go out toward Mexico. My father showed me that. We would go around Texas and then around the Mexican coast."[27]

Inshore shrimpers target whites and browns too, but also other marine forms (commercial finfish and crabs). More important, inshore shrimpers catch smaller and, therefore, less valuable shrimp. The inshore shrimping cycle is ten to twenty-four hours, interrupted by repairs, demands of family, availability of shrimp, and unexpected weather.

Table 1 (appendix B) shows that the majority of Louisiana shrimpers have resided in the State for ten or more years, have a family history with shrimping, and have friends and relatives who are also involved in shrimping. Furthermore, the majority have been recruited into the fishery through kin and see shrimping as more than just a job. They identify autonomy as the reason shrimping is attractive. Only one-fourth identify shrimping or other marine harvesting as their primary occupation, and another one-fourth report oil and related work as their primary occupation. Few count themselves as members of commercial fishing organizations, and even fewer describe themselves as highly involved with these organizations.

In many ways Louisiana's full-time shrimpers are comparable to full-time shrimpers we interviewed from other states (table 2, appendix B). They are part of an established community of harvesters whose way of life is shaped by shrimping. They too have been shrimping ten or more years, their kin and friends shrimp, they land other marine species in addition to shrimp, and they utilize their bycatch.

Studies on shrimpers from other states reinforce the findings available from the sample of non-Louisiana shrimpers. The Alabama fleet of Bayou La Batre, Alabama, is similar to the full-time shrimpers of Louisiana.[28] Similarly, South Atlantic shrimpers are comparable to their full-time Louisiana counterparts,[29] as are Oregon's shrimpers.[30]

More relevant to the effect of offshore oil on shrimping is Maril's 1983 study of Texas shrimpers.[31] Arguably, the Texas fleet comes closer to modern capitalism than its Louisiana counterpart. The Texas Shrimp Association has more influence in government circles and is better financed than the Louisiana Shrimp Association. Fleet owners are more prevalent, and the crews are most typically nonfamily wage workers. To be sure, there are fleet owners in Louisiana, but they constitute a smaller proportion of Louisiana's fleet.

The Texas fleet is ethnically different from the Louisiana fleet. Hispanics, Anglos, and African Americans are larger components of the Texas fleet that Maril studied. The Texas shrimper is younger than his Louisiana counterpart.[32] The educational level of shrimpers in Texas appears to be lower,[33] probably because of the large number of better educated recreational shrimpers holding commercial licenses in Louisiana. Texas shrimpers' attitudes about work seem to be more ambivalent.[34] However, both Texas and Louisiana shrimpers also want their children to face better conditions in the future.

On kinship connections in the fishery, Texas and Louisiana shrimpers are comparable. Most shrimpers in both studies have kin and close friends in shrimping. Yet, Maril argues: "That there are so few family-crewed boats is, again, a comment on the demanding nature of the work. To expect a father and sons, or other close family members, to work together for months at sea and then endure family relationships at home is to expect what appears to be beyond the capability of most shrimpers."[35] Among Louisiana's offshore workers, we got a different reaction. Although we did not specifically ask about the presence of kin, we did receive enough relevant information to conclude that shrimping with kin is usual. Perhaps the explanation is that Maril's sample, like the Texas offshore shrimper population from which it was drawn, is skewed toward the nonowner captain.

Finally, Maril reports that shrimpers are perceived as problem drinkers in their home communities. He argues, however, that the evidence fails to match the reality with the perception. Although we have no comparable data for Louisiana shrimpers, his comment that "shrimpers rarely drink at sea" runs counter to the beliefs we recorded from fishery managers. Yet, it is possible that fishery managers are merely reflecting a stereotype. In fact, we did not find the "wild drunks"[36] image, referred to by Maril, in Louisiana communities. Perhaps, again, he interviewed more nonowner captains and riggers and headers who were hired hands. We concluded that Louisiana crews are often composed of friends and relatives. Arguably, shrimpers in Louisiana enjoy a better reputation in their home communities than their Texas counterparts. But we believe that Louisiana shrimpers are more traditional because modernization that accompanied offshore oil development came later than it did in Texas. Furthermore, the more isolated and culturally homogeneous communities of Louisiana were better able to resist modernization. Shrimping is more clearly interwoven in the fabric of the local culture in Louisiana. Although it remains a traditional occupation in many regards, it has also changed.

Under the new social arrangements, competition over the resources accelerated. The full-time shrimper trawled more days. Many moved offshore and stayed longer at sea. Today, a shrimper/fisher may be gone for seven or eight months a year, with several trips home during this time, each trip lasting two or three weeks. The shrimper is also home during the off-season.[37] The problem with this arrangement, of course, is that it is more disruptive to the family. Thus, the nature of work itself strains family relations. The father is home so seldom that most activities focus around the mother who assumes management in his absence.[38] Although she does have help from friends and relatives, particularly her own mother whom she visits often, the wife of the shrimper is ultimately alone. On her shoulders the tasks of running the household and disciplining children rests.[39] During her husband's absence, she must not only carry out the traditional role of housewife but also respond to the daily demands that her husband might have normally handled.[40]

The woes of full-time shrimpers run deeper. They face a number of problems, illustrated in table 3 (appendix B). The fishery is overcrowded and diverse. A recreational shrimp fishery is in direct competition with full-time shrimpers. Many shrimpers can no longer afford to reduce bycatch or throw it away. A long-time shrimper offers a vivid description of how shrimping has changed: "In the late 1940s there was so much shrimp and fish in the nets that when you picked them up they would sometimes break. So we invented a Fish Excluder Device to get the fish out so there would be only shrimp and less weight. Now we have a Turtle Excluder Device, and we do not like it because we want to keep every fish and shrimp in the nets. Our earnings are so marginal we cannot afford even the smallest loss of catch."[41]

In response to the changes in shrimping, some leave the fishery, regretfully or enthusiastically. One shrimper reminisced: I have been shrimping for over forty years. My son is a shrimper. He has a seventy-foot boat. . . . [He is] a deep-water shrimper, just like I was until a year ago. He is a real shrimper, goes out for about three weeks. I finally gave it up—sold my boat."[42] Other shrimpers lament the changes but keep on shrimping:

In the late 1940s I could go out for three days, and after paying all expenses, I would have enough money to buy a car. Now I go out for two weeks, and I worry about not meeting expenses. The price of engine parts, repairs, fuel keep going up, while the price of shrimp has not kept up. I have been doing this since World War II, and my son also shrimps. Every year we seem to have less money after expenses; or put it this way, a shrimper could afford a better life years ago. . . . . their lifestyle seems to get a little lower each season.[43]

Many shrimpers and fishers stay on because they feel that they are trapped. Their way of life, once fondly embraced, becomes a burden from which they cannot escape. Many both love and hate shrimping. They turn to the sea for freedom, and, ironically, they find themselves imprisoned. Although many desire to obtain a good job onshore, most eventually return to the fishing industry. Their reasons for not leaving the occupation are numerous. Many lack the skills needed for comparable salaried onshore jobs. If they were to accept lower skilled jobs onshore, they would be unable to provide their families with as high a standard of living.[44]

CONCLUSION AND ANALYSIS

We have argued that parallel trends in shrimping and the drilling for oil offshore sped the decline in shrimping. Larger vessels and more sophisticated gear were used to shrimp deeper waters. Inevitably, the limits of nature were reached, and an increased effort was necessary to maintain previous harvest levels. Shrimping and oil work became viable work alternatives. Offshore work had high wages and benefits. Work was steady, as were the pay checks. Money from oil work supplied the capital for larger vessels for those who shrimped commercially. For others, it supported a much-loved pastime; nonetheless, because of the large number of part-time and recreational shrimpers, the shrimp stock was under increasing pressure. And this was happening at a time when shrimp imports began to put a downward pressure on shrimp prices.

Yet, other changes were in evidence. No longer were people exclusively ranked according to their talents (skill in shrimping) or familial statuses. Social rank was increasingly taking on a modern shape. For many this meant placing a greater importance on possessing things, often buying them on time.

Yet, the evidence suggests that Cajun culture has not been dismantled by the coming of offshore oil. Although in many ways Cajuns have resisted modernization, the relationships between offshore oil and the traditional culture of south Louisiana has been, at least to some extent, congenial. No other industry would have allowed the culture to survive, and no other culture would have given the industry such an accommodating workforce. Even in economically depressed times, the father's altered working pattern left the family intact. The family also remained geographically in place, not disrupting the community. Given the volatility of the oil industry, these intact communities of workers are necessary to the industry's resurgence. Likewise, the survival of this life-style is fostered by the unique work scheduling of offshore oil. In substance, cultural traits like shrimping can survive. But one cannot ignore recent research on the oil industry in Louisiana that has convincingly demonstrated that higher homicide and suicide rates accompany rapidly changing oil activity.[45] Although the causal connection between the boom-and-bust cycles of oil in Louisiana and the increases in homicides and suicides remains to be clarified, the implications are obvious. Progress comes at a price.

What are the long-term effects on traditional life-styles? Oil spawns a larger middle class with more money for recreational fishing. Therefore, proportionally fewer people harvest commercially. But before this change happens, a variety of factors lead to overfishing and intense competition for available stock. Eventually, fishing becomes more of a spare time activity, an amusement, and a respite from routine work. As fishing becomes more recreational, new interests emerge and supersede former concerns. Fishing regulations tend to become more supportive of maintaining ample stocks for recreational interests rather than for commercial harvesters.

The opportunity to marry people of a higher status is created as migrants enter the area with higher levels of education and technical skills necessary for success in the new economy. This trend tends to diminish the number of potential harvesters, as family members will be more likely to go into higher status occupations. It will also increase the number of recreational shrimpers/fishers, as individuals transform skills and equipment into recreational pastimes. Yet, those who pursue shrimping/fishing full-time face dwindling stocks and stiff competition from an expanded recreational component. They are forced to redouble their efforts to make a living.

As migrants enter an area, they also bring with them different life-styles and cultures, setting the stage for potential conflict. Eventually, cultures will change as affluent outsiders come to dominant the new social arrangements. In doing so, their cultural values gain legitimacy. Generational gaps may emerge as youth imitate these newer life-styles influences; the older customs are cast off and often perceived as inferior.

Those who currently shrimp were influenced by the higher monetary rewards and the accommodating work/family schedule. Yet, the legacy of oil has made the prospects for shrimping worse. Marshes, the nursery for fish, shrimp, and crabs, are now cut by numerous canals, making them vulnerable to sea and wind. Louisiana is losing marshland at unprecedented rates. Pollution hazards and the tear-ing-up of nets and other fishing gear are taking their toll on an occupation whose margin of profit is small. And when oil is gone, the future of shrimping is uncertain.

The inevitable exit of the oil industry in Louisiana and Texas will result in social/economic shock. Depending on how long the industry has existed determines in large part how well the community and individuals are able or willing to return to their traditional occupations. Shrimping provides a renewable resource and a continuing and growing economic and social support base. Unlike shrimping/fishing which extracts a renewable resource, the failure of extracting minerals is inevitable. But can the fisheries absorb the workers exiting the oil patch? Can the environmental damage to marshes and water quality be remedied?

Historically, industrialization has been incompatible with traditionalism.[46] The interplay of offshore oil and Acadian culture perhaps creates some exceptions, but eventually it is generally negative. The scars left behind are not simply the carved up marshes but the fragmented lives as well. Others have pondered the effect drilling for offshore oil has had on fishing:

> Yet for the moment, the romance of fishing as a way of life remains attractive to enough young men who enjoy the traditional skills of seamanship, the camaraderie, and the freedom from clocks and bosses to ensure the survival of fishing in Burra on some scale well into the future. Indeed, if the strategy of minimum risk succeeds and fishing survives through the oil era to the end of the century, it may regain its past preeminence. The danger is, however, that fishing as a way of life, a virtue borne of generations of necessity, may have become eroded and debased as necessity has vanished. In the interval, expectations and aspirations will have changed. It may be too late to turn back. It is still too early to know how the decline and possible disappearance of fishing, so central to the spirit, culture and identity of Burra people, will affect the way they think about their society, and how they will behave as members of it.[47]

Two judgments have been made as the spirit of modernism erodes traditions: one laments the passing away of the old; the other celebrates the arrival of the new. If one assumes that the traditional life is beautiful, one could argue that capitalism/rationalism has brought long-term detriment to these communities. In short, this judgement laments the death of a way of life. "They are pulled into the money economy, their members are transformed from independent commodity producers to wage labor, their self-sufficiency is eroded, their heritage of skills and knowledge foregone, and when the whole era ends (as it will in the lifetime of those now alive) they will not have the capacity to re-establish their former lifestyles."[48]

The key assumption in the defense of traditionalism is that if traditional society were to remain isolated, it would survive. But this ignores the benefits of the penetration of industrialization and modernization. Furthermore, both change and stability are two-edged swords. Traditionalism limits freedom and modernism undermines stability. "There is no question that penetration releases people, provides some with new choices and new opportunities to use talents which had no value in the simpler society. It releases men and women from predetermined lifestyles, work, marital patterns, and family obligations. The process is neither wholly good nor bad, and judging it in simple terms is somewhat like judging the first industrial revolution."[49]

We are mindful that we should not attempt to romanticize Acadian culture, and we have tried to resist that temptation,[50] as have the Cajuns themselves. As one long-time resident of Acadia told us:

> I use to be a farmer. I inherited a small farm from my father. Farming is hard work. When I started shrimping it was easier than farming and I liked being out there on the water. In the 1960s I went to work offshore. Now I still live on a farm, and I still have a boat I keep to shrimp in during my spare time. But I don't earn a living from those two things. I prefer to work offshore. The money is good and steady. Anybody who wants to farm or shrimp for a living either has never worked on a farm or shrimped for a living. There may be something romantic about drinking a cup of coffee at daybreak, while looking out over the water or farm land, but that is where it stops. Working in the oil industry has allowed me to have farming and shrimping as a pastime, and that is where I want to keep it. None of my sons are farmers or shrimpers, and none of my daughters married one. . . . I feel my children and [we] have better lives now.[51]

Society is not static. The general trend and most important type of social change that has occurred and is still in progress is the change from simple, traditional, agricultural societies to highly complex, rational, industrial ones. In this book we have tried to focus on the consequences of social change for Acadia. We have tried to chronicle the changes and describe the negative and positive consequences of change. But, most importantly, we have tried to show the interconnection of oil and shrimp. The spirit modernity introduced by the intrusion of oil set the stage for the TEDS conflict over shrimp and turtles.

Chapter

3

Blockades and Protests

From 1989 to 1991 angry shrimpers staged or threatened protest actions. Some of these actions were legal protests over TEDS regulations, others involved illegal blockades of waterways.

After numerous delays and within hours of the scheduled enforcement of TEDS regulations in July of 1989, shipping lanes along the Texas and Louisiana coasts were blockaded. In succeeding days and weeks, other protests and blockades staged by angry shrimpers made their displeasure over TEDS very clear. But these actions were smaller and more localized expressions of discontent than the weekend blockades of July 22–23 in 1989.

The plan promoted by Concerned Shrimpers of America called for shrimpers from Florida to Texas to head directly to the closest harbor the moment a signal was given. Typically in July, the majority of shrimpers would be off the coasts of Louisiana and Texas; therefore, only Louisiana and Texas ports would be affected. CSA was unsuccessful in getting the smaller South Atlantic fleet to take similar action in the Atlantic.

On July 22, the date that marked the start of the blockades, the bulk of the shrimping fleet was off the central coast of Texas. CSA leaders had previously consulted the Coast Guard to get clearance for a parade of vessels.[1] The focus of the protest would be at Galveston. CSA President Tee John Mialjevich was to personally coordinate the protest there. Wilma Anderson, vice president of CSA, was to stay at Aransas to coordinate what was expected to be a smaller contingent of shrimpers. Other CSA members or officials were to coordinate activities in Louisiana.

CSA's objectives were to show unity, express its resolve to fight TEDS, and get favorable press coverage. Shrimpers believed that the press would be as sympathetic to the shrimpers as it had been to civil rights activists. Shrimpers saw themselves as underdogs fighting for their rights just as the civil rights activists had. But the press was not favorable and operations did not develop as planned.

A Louisiana protester provided this account of the unexpected events and last minute changes:

> I was asked by Tee John to be prepared to go by helicopter to Galveston and help keep the peace there. We had been having some meetings, and it had been decided that Louisiana and Texas would do the protest at the same time, but the Coast Guard had been harassing some shrimpers in Texas, and the Texas people said, "Let's go [ahead with the blockade]", and we didn't know if we would be ready in Louisiana. That's why I was asked to go to Galveston. Tee John was going to have the helicopter pick me up in my backyard. At the last minute the Louisiana protest happened on a big scale, and Tee John decided that it be best that I deal with the press and with communications, so I ended up making three trips by helicopter to Grand Isle.[2]

In Louisiana angry shrimpers assembled at Cameron, Intracoastal City, and Grand Isle. In Texas, chiefly at Galveston (Houston ship channel) and Aransas Pass (Corpus Christi), the largest contingent of shrimpers converged on shipping lanes. In fewer numbers at Freeport and Brownsville, Texas, shrimpers blockaded shipping lanes. Estimates varied, but as many as four hundred vessels blockaded passes at Aransas. At Galveston the same number of vessels held up marine traffic. In each of the other affected locations, fifty to one hundred vessels actively participated. In most of the blockaded passes, numerous smaller vessels gave moral support to the blockading shrimpers. In all, about one thousand vessels actively participated in the blockade. Another thousand smaller vessels gave moral support to blockading shrimpers.

TROUBLE AT GALVESTON AND ARANSAS

The strategic center of area covered by the blockade was Galveston. On July 22 a Coast Guard radar operator reported hundreds of blips on the screen that appeared to be converging on Galveston Bay. Shortly thereafter, according to one eyewitness, an excited Coast Guard call came in: "There's over four hundred blips on our screen. What the hell is going on?"[3]

What was supposed to be a peaceful protest became a blockade of one of the busiest seaways in the world, the Houston ship channel. The Galveston blockade was potentially the most disruptive to commercial shipping interests. But ferry traffic to the island city of Galveston was also halted by the blockade.

At Aransas more vessels than the CSA expected blockaded three passes. Wilma Anderson was alone to arbitrate peace between the Coast Guard and the angry shrimpers. One protester who was present reported on the chaotic conditions:

> I was in the protest in Aransas Pass. We were trying to block the channel. We anchored in the channel. The young Coast Guardsmen seemed to be having a good time cutting our anchor ropes. They were acting unprofessionally. They used fire hoses to break us up. It was a miracle that no one got hurt. There was only minor damage [from cutting anchor ropes on shrimping vessels so closely lined up in a channel with a strong current]. [The protest lasted] twenty-four hours or less—one whole morning. [Despite Coast Guard interference, the shrimpers regrouped.] That night the tide shifted and some anchor ropes broke. . . . Sometime the next day Mosbacher or some government people came and promised to look into the matter, and we moved out. [There were] about five hundred [boats]. Smaller vessels were anchored in the port. They came for the protest but were too small to block the channel. A fleet from Brownsville showed up the next morning. We were all shrimping, and you were supposed to go to the nearest place. I was fishing off south Texas.[4]

Shrimp trawlers maneuvered their vessels across the affected channels and anchored side by side to create a formidable physical barrier, three or four vessels deep. The shrimpers tried to hold their formations against tidal changes and strong currents. At Aransas and Galveston the Coast Guard used water cannons to disperse the shrimpers. Guardsmen directed their water cannons into the stacks to flood the engines. In some instances mooring lines were cut by guardsmen or snapped by tidal changes. Shrimpers responded by fastening their vessels to adjacent vessels with the small metal cables used to raise trawls.

Each side in the fray recorded the dramatic events. The Coast Guard photographed the vessels involved and used the pictures to bring charges against some of the participants. The shrimpers videotaped what they considered the unprofessional behavior of the Coast Guard.

The standoff between guardsmen and shrimpers lasted thirty-six hours at Galveston and fewer hours at Aransas. Nonetheless, the protest continued.

In September of 1989 shrimpers protested along the parade route of President George Bush's visit to the area. They also picketed the *Times-Picayune*'s main office to protest what they felt was that newspaper's biased coverage of the blockades, and they staged a blockade of vessels at Grand Isle, Louisiana. Many openly defied the TEDS regulations during the 1990 shrimping season. In July of 1991 shrimpers met to plan a mass act of civil disobedience. They wanted to call attention to their problems by shrimping en masse without TEDS during the largest fishing rodeo held in Louisiana, the Grand Isle Tarpon Rodeo.[5] This planned protest did not materialize, and Concerned Shrimpers of America dissolved in 1992. Whether these events portend the end of protests or the emergence of less organized and, therefore, potentially more violent protests, is unclear. What is certain is that the TEDS protest (the blockades and other collective acts of resistance) has had a significant impact on all parties to the resource dispute. But how did one segment of middle America come to protest and violate criminal law, actions which this group usually abhors?

Since the 1960s a number of protests and social movements have appeared on the American scene. The civil rights, feminists, environmental, and other social movements have significantly altered American social arrangements.

Typically social movements push for change or a return to a previous and supposedly better state of affairs. The TEDS protest is an interesting example of the latter. We see the TEDS protest as a collection of both planned and unplanned events. And we are more interested in communicating the complexity of the drama and the difficulties encountered in trying to explain it.

Explanations of protests either stress social-psychological states (discontent) that individuals collectively experience or the power relations that a group desires to change. Unfortunately, we have no single explanation that embraces both dimensions in a satisfactory way. The TEDS protest illustrates both dimensions and is far richer than the theories available to explain it.

To oversimplify, protests and mass actions are either explained as the irrational acts of individuals prone to follow so-called holy causes or the cool calculations of those who know how to get and use resources to change what they do not like. Long scholarly traditions stand behind these contrasting visions.[6] Yet, we have heard the TEDS players propose comparable contrasting explanations.

CONTRASTING VISIONS

Classical explanations of social movements stress the abnormality of participants, or extremists. But what kind of people become extremists? Lipset claims that "miners, fishermen, lumbermen, and one-crop farmers are prone to the extremism on the left because of their income insecurity."[7] He continues, "Extremist movements have much in common. They appeal to the disgruntled and the psychologically homeless, to the personal failures, the socially isolated, the economically insecure, the uneducated, unsophisticated, and authoritarian persons at every level of the society."[8]

Society often assigns irrationality to actors so that their actions are seen as products of primitive psychological dispositions. Protest behavior is spontaneous, unstructured, and uncritical. The actions of crowds are not planned or contrived but spread like a contagious disease.[9] The reflexive dimension in social behavior is missing.[10] Protest behavior is the action of the impatient.[11] Alienation, grievances, and deprivations are objectively true or genuinely subjectively felt to be true.[12]

This vision of protest behavior was born out of the concern for global, social, and political stability—fascism and Communism in Europe, Latin America, and Asia—and focused on extremism as the major threat to that stability.

By contrast, a more contemporary vision blossomed from the experiences of American movements in the 1960s and 1970s which saw a variety of disaffected and alienated groups attempt to change society with varying degrees of success. A sufficiently large number of individuals, both volunteers and paid professionals, became a pool of "movement entrepreneurs" from which future movements could draw.[13] Knowledge of mobilizing people and resources became a problem in technology transfer. Movement professionals were sought after to ply their skills at engineering movements. Skills and technology acquired through working on one problem could be used to solve new social problems. With sufficient funds and a core of professional organizers, more funds, recruits, and even grievances could be mobilized.[14] In the social environment which allowed movement technology to score success after success, new theories were offered to represent the "new reality." Traditional theories were discarded in the wake of the successes of contemporary movements. New ideas and policies were incorporated into the fabric of society. It was no longer possible to think of the new power groups as extremists.

The new vision proclaimed: (1) a protester is a rational actor who can be swayed by rational arguments of self-interest; (2) movements are resource-dependent. One of the most important resources is organization. Actions of movement adherents must be organized, planned, and choreographed to be effective; (3) grievances and whatever emotions adherents feel must be carefully orchestrated to be effective; (4) the political process and access to it are crucial to the success of social movements; and finally (5) change or resistance to change is guided and nurtured by those who have the resources or who can mobilize the necessary resources and bring these to the political arena.

COMPETING PREDICTIONS

The traditional way of viewing protesters would suggest that shrimpers are prone to extremism on a number of accounts. They are uneducated, culturally homogeneous, and socially isolated. Furthermore, they are entrepreneurs (petit bourgeois) very similar to one-crop farmers.[15] Extremism from the left should have a special appeal for fishers, particularly in Louisiana, home of a populist movement under the political dynasty of the Longs.[16] As a result, shrimpers of Louisiana should be open to a charismatic leader who promises deliverance from their troubles. Following the same logic, one would also think that as unsophisticated people, shrimpers should be responsive to organized labor and be good followers. Finally, one should expect evidence of irrationality as extremists vent their anger. In short, grievances should be deeply felt, not whipped up or contrived for public relations purposes. By contrast, the contemporary vision suggests a quite different set of predictions.

It emphasizes resources, particularly organizations (in this case, Concerned Shrimpers of America). The political process and power relations are crucial to the success of movements.[17] More formality, centralization, and continuity with institutional patterns are emphasized. One expects a bit more sophistication, more organization, more evidence of coordination with other organizations, and an effective use of the political process. Furthermore, one should expect not only political sophistication, but a demonstration of skill at mobilizing political power. Finally, there should be evidence of reliance on movement professionals and contrivance of grievances for public consumption.

An examination of the TEDS protest reveals actions that are both planned and spontaneous, rational and irrational. We will make no attempt to force the TEDS protest to fit one vision or another.

ANALYSIS OF PROTEST ACTIONS

Because of shrimpers' actions in 1989 and 1990, middle America came to identify them as protesters and criminals, a public image that bothered many shrimpers. But even today many still feel the same contempt towards the TEDS protest and its outcome as they felt in the summer of 1989: "That was not the way to do it [protest]. They [shrimpers] created attention. They created problems by breaking the law. They were endangering lives," said an old Cajun shrimper.[18] "We fought and blockaded everything, but no one helped but only the shrimper. We blocked the canal, but we get no help from the government, and some of the protestors have to go to jail," remarked a Vietnamese shrimper.[19]

Discontent of some form or another is commonplace, but dissatisfaction over a particular issue often never develops beyond complaints. Malaise often remains diffused and unfocused. Collective action follows discontent only if the aggrieved individuals collectively identify the source of the problem and its solution. Collective actions are taken if discontent is salient and the proposed action (i.e., the blockade) is considered both legitimate and efficacious. In other words, in order for shrimpers to have blockaded they had to believe that the TEDS issue was important, blockading harbors was justified, and that these actions would produce results.

SALIENCY

Long before the 1989 blockade, shrimpers publicly opposed TEDS. Not surprisingly, 99 percent (table 4, appendix B) of the shrimpers we interviewed agreed with the statement that "TEDS are a threat to my way of life." Furthermore, the majority agreed with the protest and felt the shrimpers did not endanger turtles (table 5, appendix B). Although no one doubts that shrimpers hate TEDS, it is difficult to understand why.

To communicate their feelings, shrimpers have linked TEDS with other controversial issues. In coastal Louisiana roadside signs exhort, "Abort TEDS, not babies." The underlying message is to link what the community takes to be less serious (TEDS) with what it considers a grave matter (abortion). But its the shrimpers' actions that deserve notice, and their behavior towards TEDS reveals both fear and anger.

One marine agent recalled the behavior of a group of shrimpers when they first encountered TEDS at a meeting. "They encircled it, staring at it, then touching it, and quickly withdrawing as if it were a snake."[20] Another marine agent who had brought his TED-fitted trawl to demonstrate TEDS to potential adopters had his net torched. Not only do the shrimpers despise TEDS, they cite economic reasons for their dissatisfaction. But was the issue serious enough to warrant a blockade?

LEGITIMACY AND EFFICACY

Even though most shrimpers agreed with the protest, some had serious doubts over whether the blockade was justified and whether the actions would produce results. Nonprotesters commented, "I think that [the blockade] was wrong." Interestingly, others said the same thing but added, "I didn't agree with it [the blockade], but it called attention to the problem." But protesters themselves seemed to have mixed feelings. "We had to do something," said many who agreed with the protest. Still, there were those who, without reservations, affirmed the action. "I thought it was great and wished that I could have been there. We talked about doing something here [North Carolina], but that's all it ended up being, talk."[21] "Yeah, it's time to get our views in the public knowledge", said a Georgia shrimper. He added, "I agree to [sic] the protests as long as they are nonviolent."[22] A North Carolina shrimper remarked, "Yeah, we sent [protesters] from here." But was it worth it? "Well, I would say yes. To show that the fishery industry was not going to sit around and take everything without a show of unity."[23]

Although the majority agreed with the blockades and unanimously hated TEDS, their feelings were mixed on whether the blockades were right and worth doing.

The blockades and protests were planned, but the anger displayed by the shrimpers was spontaneous. The deeply felt emotions evoked by TEDS enveloped the plan and threatened to undermine it. It is obvious that TEDS were demonized and came to symbolize everything wrong in the fishery.

TEDS is a drama, and dramatic events are scripted. It is necessary for performances to be embellished to ensure audience response. That is, actions and emotions can be contrived in a calculating way. But even a choreographed performance, to be successful, must tap real emotions.[24]

The shrimpers wanted to orchestrate events for maximum effect. They wanted the press to tell the public about their plight, and they felt that strong actions were necessary to protest such an injustice. Their words came from spontaneous desperation but gave rise to calculated acts. The closer we examined the core of leadership, the clearer the image of designed collective actions became. According to one protester:

> After the teds [regulations] were passed, shrimpers were discouraged. The protests helped quite a bit. The [blockades] helped the most, especially when the Intracoastal was blocked, because [President] Bush owns a big part of Hollywood Marine, which owns a large part of the towboats and oil terminals on the Waterway. Hollywood Marine is one of the biggest on the Intracoastal Waterway. When the oil industry went bust and the small independents had to get out, Hollywood Marine bought them out cheap to where now they are about the only towing company [in the area]. . . . Every other boat was a Hollywood Marine boat, and we told the ship captains [of the blocked towboats] to tell the company to tell their owner Bush that we wanted to talk to him when he [came] to New Orleans. [The President was scheduled to visit the area.][25]

The collective actions were planned exclusively by the leadership of Concerned Shrimpers of America, at a time when the leaders included shrimpers from North Carolina to Texas. Long before 1989, CSA spoke for those who shrimped for a living. Besides Tee John, its founder and president, CSA had talented leaders from the Texas Shrimp Association as well as leaders from other state and local shrimper groups to help plan and execute a strategy of resistance to TEDS. Even though a majority of shrimpers knew how the protest was organized (table 4), a substantial proportion heard about it from the mass media, rather than from CSA. Clearly, CSA was unable to mobilize all the discontented.

MOBILIZING AND ORGANIZING THE UNORGANIZABLE

To explain how CSA mobilized shrimpers requires an appreciation of the resources that had to be mobilized. Resources included: (1) change technology, (2) finances, (3) communication networks, (4) organization, and (5) ideology.

CHANGE TECHNOLOGY

Change technology refers to those skills necessary to use the political process to foster one's agenda. This includes, but is not limited to, knowledge of the political process, lobbying, giving testimony in hearings and in courts, presenting data to panels and agencies and the like. Without a professional staff of lawyers and lobbyists, shrimpers had to play these roles themselves. Yet the majority of full-time shrimpers have little education and a low tolerance for formal groups, such as unions. Therefore, no union professional staff was available to them. They did not have the services of movement professionals that so many movements of the 1960s and 1970s had. They did, however, have some talented and educated women (wives and daughters) who not only managed family businesses but made substantial contributions to organizing shrimpers and mobilizing communities. But there were far too few of them available. Ironically, it was the federal government that transferred the change technology to shrimpers, which was ultimately used by shrimpers to resist federal regulations.

Sea Grant Extension Service gave shrimpers the technology to change laws. This included leadership training and other skills necessary to influence the political process. Since the middle of the 1970s, marine agents had been providing technical and general information useful to marine harvesters. But through their newsletters and workshops, they were also teaching them how to communicate their grievances to state government and lobby for change. Because marine agents "did teach them how to lobby at Austin,"[26] an unintended consequence was that these newly acquired skills were used to resist regulations promulgated by the federal government. In short, NOAA, through its Sea Grant Program, provided the change technology which shrimpers used in their struggle against TEDs. Change technology alone is not sufficient to organize an effective movement; an adequate funding base is also needed.

FINANCES

In hindsight it is easy to identify one of the fundamental weaknesses of the shrimpers' movement. From the beginning, shrimpers did not have adequate funding to ensure a successful challenge to TEDs, perhaps because their independent nature prevented them from asking and accepting outside money. CSA depended on the two-hundred-dollar annual dues, so limited finances was probably not a serious problem in the early protest stage. Many shrimpers had done well economically in the 1970s and 1980s. One shrimper queried, "What kind of job do you know where you go out cold broke and in a single day return with $1000 in your pocket?"[27] Interestingly, 1986 was a very good year, and shrimpers had a bumper harvest. But shrimp harvests declined, and prices went down in response to increasing foreign imports. By the spring of 1992, evidence of a weak financial base was apparent. Tee John Mialjevich took an onshore job, and lack of funding curtailed travel for Tee John and others in the movement. The challenge to TEDs, at least from CSA, was over. But from 1986 until its disbanding, CSA effectively mobilized political forces against TEDS. This challenge could not have been possible without an effective communication network.

Shrimpers relied on two vehicles to establish effective communications—one is old, the other new. The personal and familial ties in every fishing village along the coast unites shrimpers in a community based on a common culture, life-style, and, in some cases, ethnicity. Shrimpers congregate on the docks and share advice on shrimping and exchange ideas on everything from the national news to local gossip. These casual gatherings are as important to shrimpers as their time at sea because it satisfies the most basic of human needs, a sense of belonging. It is an intrinsic part of what makes shrimping a way of life. It is also a network through which messages can travel quickly. To be inside that network is to know what all others in the network know and to identify oneself with the collective "we." While closed to nonharvesters, the network of shrimpers articulates with the larger community through kinship, propinquity, and shared values and beliefs. Thus, shrimpers are tied to their home communities, and the network of shrimpers interlocks with the larger community. The more unified and isolated the community, the more parochial its members.

In Louisiana each bay seems to create its own community or cluster of communities. Historically, harvesters generally remained in their home bay. With the advent of larger vessels and the arrival of newcomers, the isolation of former times was broken. The result has been to broaden the community of shrimpers. Nonetheless, there still is a great deal of older parochial spirit. However, the network of shrimpers or, more accurately, the network of shrimper networks is an effective system of communication, particularly among offshore shrimpers. By contrast, many inshore shrimpers appear to be out of the direct loop with the larger shrimper community that cuts across village, bay, and state boundaries. The most convincing evidence of exclusion is that more inshore shrimpers heard about the protest from the mass media (table 4).

The effective network of shrimpers was made more effective by the introduction of marine radios. With their marine radios, shrimpers have not only kept in touch with family and fellow shrimpers but also made last minute coordinations before the blockade. During the blockades, the radio was indispensable for communicating instructions. And it was over the radio that shrimpers heard the message to end the protest.

In a short period of time, Tee John focused the anger of shrimpers from North

Carolina to Texas on TEDS. Considering the logistical problems, not to mention the barriers of provincialism, what he accomplished was a coup de grace. The technique Tee John used was simple and direct. A marine agent described it as if it were an everyday occurrence. "When I gave talks about TEDS in [the] early 1980s, Tee John asked to accompany me. When I had finished, he would get up and talk about Concerned Shrimpers of America. This was when he was organizing it."[28] Tee John used those meetings, planned and financed by the government to introduce shrimpers to TEDS, to launch a new organization of shrimpers. In doing so, Tee John was emulating labor unions that have historically used the industries they represent as a labor-organizing device. His immediate purpose was to convince them to resist TEDS. All of the logistical problems of meeting with shrimpers from eight states extending over hundreds of miles of coastline were solved by agencies of the federal government. Tee John soon convinced hundreds of shrimpers that they could resist the use of TEDS if they organized. But to actually accomplishing that goal, an effective organization had to pull shrimpers together and coordinate their actions. From influencing the state government of Louisiana, to forbidding the enforcement of TEDS in state waters, to a legal challenge of TEDS in the federal courts, the organizational effectiveness of CSA was evident. In some measure CSA's effectiveness came from its charismatic leader, but the "Jesus of shrimpers," as one critic called Tee John, could not do it alone.

CSA was also strengthened by its organizational ties with local and regional shrimper organizations. CSA did not attempt to discredit the older organizations. In fact, officeholders of existing shrimper associations were placed on the CSA board. In areas without formally organized associations, CSA created local chapters. The organization combined the integrating effectiveness of an umbrella organization with the direct contact principle of the town meeting. Concerns of individual shrimpers could be handled through their representative on the CSA board or directly from the floor at general meetings. From 1986 through 1989, when it organized the blockades and protests, it was a unifying force and the only hope for redress for thousands of shrimpers. During its lifetime, CSA not only mobilized shrimpers but also created a powerful ideology that contributed to the solidarity of shrimpers.

IDEOLOGY

Ideologies function to unite otherwise detached discontented souls in a common bond of pain. By identifying the source of discontent, the ideology supplies the aggrieved with a common enemy. United by a shared ideology, the discontented are able to explain their predicament and develop a collective solution. For shrimpers TEDS were a unifying force. But shrimpers went beyond seeing TEDS as unfair or senseless; they constructed an ideology that explained the emergence of TEDS. In its most distilled form, this ideology argued that TEDS and other regulations (proposed bycatch regulations to reduce the amount of finfish shrimpers catch while trawling) are attempts by powerful elites to rid U.S. waters of commercial harvesters. Although these issues are explored in subsequent chapters, they are mentioned here to identify the content of the ideology that helped unify shrimpers. The relevant point is that shrimpers perceived the rich and powerful elite as their enemy. In contrast, the shrimpers perceived themselves as the underdog.

But shrimpers could only fight the enemy by the rules laid out by government. The rule makers were not merely officials in the game, but they were also drawn into the conflict. And government provided the area on which the conflict was staged.

Chapter

4

States, Government Agencies, and Mediation

The TEDS conflict illustrates how social movements—the environmental movement and the shrimpers' protest—both affected and were effected by government. The TEDS story shows how interest groups access the power of government and, in turn, how government agencies variably resist or cooperate with emerging power brokers.

In this chapter, we will examine (1) the responses of the affected state governments to TEDS; (2) the roles various state agencies played and are playing in the TEDS conflict at the federal level; (3) the mediation attempts taken by the federal government, which had the unintended consequence of exacerbating the TEDS conflict; and (4) the official and unofficial roles played by the Gulf Council.

THE STATES' RESPONSES TO TEDS

If one were to draw a continuum that represented reception of TEDS by state governments, Florida would probably be placed at one end and Louisiana at the other. Florida initiated TEDS regulations in state waters before federal regulations were implemented. Louisiana, by contrast, fought TEDS in the courts and implemented laws that prohibited the enforcement of the federal regulations by state agencies. Between these two opposites, the responses of the other affected states can be located. For example, congressional opposition to TEDS from the respective states fought for the fishing interests of Texas, Mississippi, Alabama, Georgia, and North and South Carolina.

But only in Louisiana was the State fully mobilized to resist TEDS. One obvious reason is that the economic and political stakes were higher in Louisiana than elsewhere. The shrimp fishery of Louisiana is critical to the State's economy. Commercial fisheries are simply larger and economically more important to Louisiana than are the fisheries of other Gulf and South Atlantic states.[1] Furthermore, proportionately more people make their living from shrimping either directly or indirectly in Louisiana than in the other states. The governor of Louisiana, Edwin Edwards, and other elected officials found it necessary to defend the State from TEDS. Even after the reform governor, Buddy Roemer, took office in 1988, State agencies were responsive to shrimping interests. An old-line agency, Louisiana Wildlife and Fisheries continued its long-standing procommercial relationship with the shrimpers. Under Roemer's reform government, the new appointees, such as Virginia Van Sickle and Jerry Clark of the Department of Environmental Quality, were not very popular with Louisiana Wildlife and Fisheries people and the commercial harvesting interests they served. They were looked upon as outsiders, although their most serious flaw may have been an inability to communicate a procommercial image. Jerry Clark, who represented the State's interests on the Gulf Council, could not win the support and confidence of commercial interests. In the course of a conversation one night after day-long meetings connected with the Council, he appeared philosophical about being replaced. He was resigned to the fact that if elected, former Governor Edwards would replace the "guy from Texas" [Jerry Clark].[2] Actually, Clark grew up in a small town in the Midwest and worked with Texas Parks and Wildlife before his appointment to his Louisiana post.

After a rather stormy election that attracted considerable interest around the world, largely because of the strong support former Ku Klux Klansman David Duke mobilized, Edwin Edwards was reelected to a fourth term. In the 1992 election Edwards got his traditional support from Louisiana Cajuns, the largest ethnic group in commercial shrimping. Edwards also received, as expected, strong support from African Americans. Enough white conservatives were frightened by the prospect of having Duke as governor to deal Edwards a decisive win in the election. Almost immediately after the election, a recall petition was initiated against Edwards. The governor did not command the popular support he enjoyed during his previous terms as governor. His reappointment of Corky Perrett as number-one person in Wildlife and Fisheries was, however, popular among commercial harvesters. Perrett served in this capacity during the previous terms of Governor Edwards and former Governor Treen. Under long-time civil servants like Perrett and others, Wildlife and Fisheries has been responsive to commercial harvesters, and commercial harvesting interests have enjoyed access to the State through Wildlife and Fisheries in much the same way that trade unions have access to the federal government through the Department of Labor. Although during former Governor Buddy Roemer's tenure some appointments of recreational fishing leaders were made, it is not likely that the influence of commercial harvesters will be lost. In fact, Governor Edwards appointed Tee John Mialjevich to the Wildlife and Fisheries Commission in 1992.[3] Considering the economic and political stakes Louisiana has in commercial harvesting, one need not look much further to explain the State's response to TEDS and its readiness to protect commercial harvesters. By contrast, Florida's commercial harvesting interests do not enjoy the same access to state government as Louisiana's harvesters do.

An analysis of Florida's land and water policy reveals the influence of that State's important recreational and tourists interests.[4] Not surprisingly, commercial harvesters have less influence in Florida than sportfishing interests. Both economically and politically, Florida's commercial harvesters are less important, since sportfishing is a significant dimension of Florida's recreational and tourist industry. In championing TEDS Florida was serving the interests of its recreational industry. Inasmuch as the regulations hurt commercial shrimpers, they help sportfishing. The two are in competition, but governments have their own interests to serve.

THE VARIOUS GOALS OF THE FEDERAL GOVERNMENT

Congress pursued both the goal of protecting turtles and protecting the industry. The history of the amendments to the Endangered Species Act clearly points to this conclusion. Congress repeatedly vacillated, alternately relaxing and strengthening protection. Its actions both in committee and on the floor can best be summarized as political compromise.

The federal government generally pursued goals that were sometimes in harmony and other times at cross-purposes. For example, one way for government to mitigate the impact of TEDS on domestic shrimpers is to restrict, tax, or limit the importation of shrimp, paralleling the restrictions American automobile manufacturers would like to see on Japanese carmakers. In the TEDS case, requiring foreign shrimpers to use TEDS as a precondition for importation to the United States would, according to domestic shrimpers, make the playing field a bit more even. Not surprisingly, shrimpers found support for this position in the halls of Congress. Louisiana Senator Bennett Johnston told a gathering of shrimpers, "You are entitled to be mad and not to take it anymore. Who required TEDS? The Department of Commerce—the Republicans! . . . Be mad at Mosbacher, a Bush appointee. . . . [The] Johnston bill requires foreign countries to impose some regulations as in the U.S. or [their shrimp will] not [be] allowed in the market."[5]

Apart from the problem of enforcement, bills aimed at forcing foreign shrimp-ers to use TEDs could hardly be fully championed by the State Department. For-eign policy goals require that the U.S. support, not hinder, the economic progress of developing countries. Because economic stability is an important determinant of political stability, we can expect the State Department to be reluctant to sup-port any measure that might undermine its foreign policy goals. These goals are clearly reflected in the assistance, both financial and technical, the United States provided to Third World countries toward the development of aquaculture (shrimp farms).

What the shrimpers got when they asked for help against imports were words, not action. Forcing TEDs on all importers was simply not feasible. Furthermore, since the majority of imports are not caught by foreign trawlers, but raised on shrimp farms nurtured by U.S. generosity, the point is moot. Not surprisingly, the differences between the wishes of Congress and the goals of the State Department in this instance produced no interbranch fight.[6] On the other hand, divergent agency goals did produce visible conflict between the National Marine Fisheries Service and Sea Grant Extension Service.

INTERAGENCY RELATIONS

The early history of NMFS reveals that this agency played a prominent service role toward commercial fishers. The regulatory role was less developed. The Magnuson Act and historical changes in coastal use patterns created a need to reshuffle roles. When the NMFS was called upon to play regulatory roles, it yielded most of its service roles to the Sea Grant Extension Service. Meanwhile, an environmental movement became institutionalized and drew broad support from corporate America. By the 1970s leisure, tourist, and recreational interests expanded in coastal America and supported coastal land and water use plans that often conflicted with commercial fishery interests.[7] Both the national environmental community and recreational fishing interests developed agendas that affected commercial fishers. At the same time, armed with the ESA, FWS aggressively championed the cause of environmentalists and conservationists and became an outspoken critic of NMFS's record on protecting and recovering species under the ESA. The fact that FWS does not routinely play a service role for commercial clients is relevant to the stance it has taken vis-à-vis NMFS. For its part, NMFS and its parent agency NOAA are mandated to offer service to the commercial sector. It is understand-able that the service roles impact the regulatory and protective roles. The conflict between the service roles and the regulatory/protective ones is an important part of the interagency conflict that developed between NMFS and Sea Grant Exten-sion Service.

The nature of this tension is well known to officials in both agencies. Basically, each agency has a somewhat divergent view of its respective role. The general assessment of career officials of each agency is that when commercial harvesters are in general agreement with management, NMFS and Sea Grant work satisfactorily. However, in conflict conditions when regulations are challenged, the relationship between the two agencies is strained.

The associate director of the Louisiana Sea Grant College Program, Ron Becker, described the mission and workings of the program during our initial examinations of the TEDS conflict. He touched on the difficulties marine agents face and the tension between the Sea Grant Extension Service and NMFS:

> Marine agents walk a tightrope; they take [what can be construed as] an oath that they will not take advocacy positions. They're in the community, yet not of the community, similar to a priest. They work sometimes with industry leaders and teach them how to present testimony and exercise parliamentary skills and leadership. . . . Marine agents are educators, but work with people where they live. . . . [They] are not expected to work with shrimpers just to push compliance with regulations [for example, TEDS]. NMFS would probably like our marine agents to work entirely on compliance and lay off the leadership development stuff. . . .[8]

When asked about the friction between the two agencies, Becker continued, "[There is] no real friction, at least until TEDS [regulations were introduced]. . . NMFS sees marine agents as federal employees. . . . They (NMFS) would like to lean on Sea Grant to lean on agents to get the shrimpers to conform." Becker added that "most marine agents believe that their credibility and effectiveness as educators would be diminished if they were to take a strong advocacy position. . . . Their inclination is to wait for the teachable moment when shrimpers themselves recognize a need for assistance with TEDS."

It is not surprising then that marine agents experienced role conflict as they were asked to transfer a technology with which they had little sympathy. Not only their clients, the shrimpers, but their home communities had come to associate TEDS with a threat to their way of life; therefore, shrimpers expected agents to take a stand against TEDS. At the same time, NMFS officials wanted agents to encourage the use of TEDS. Marine agents generally felt they were between two powerful forces. One agent succinctly summarized what being a marine agent was like amid considerable pressure from shrimpers to be their champion: "[We are] change agents, change advocates, providers of information and support. . . . It's a very difficult role [to play] in the TEDS case. They [the shrimpers] want us to say things we cannot say." Asked if the agents felt caught in the middle between the shrimpers pulling one way and the NMFS pulling the other, he agreed but added, "We can't do that [be an advocate or supporter]. We lose our effectiveness. We are part of the community. We marry into it; our friends are here. The shrimpers' best interests are served when the agent acts in an objective way. The shrewd ones know that, and they don't expect us to violate the rules."[9] Another agent underscored the difficulty of being neutral: "Our boss made it clear that no one was to discuss TEDS. This [directive occurred] right after Mosbacher came out, suspended the regs, hired [William] Fox [director of NMFS], and reimposed them. Our newsletter was a mess with this off-again, on-again regulations." When asked if the NMFS ever applied pressure, he claimed that "with the snapper fishermen, a NMFS agent tried to intimidate me into doing something [making fishermen abide by the regulations]."[10] Another agent complained that NMFS asked him to encourage the use of TEDS to unwilling shrimpers. He said, "During the voluntary period, I felt we were being asked to push TEDS. I know some of the NMFS people see our role this way. This is asking too much of us. How can I push TEDS when the state I live in and work in outlawed enforcement of them? We have to live with these guys [shrimpers]. I can't lie to them and still be all the things I'm supposed to be as an agent."[11]

Perhaps a high-ranking Sea Grant official put it best when he suggested that NMFS "had a tiger by the tail and were running around trying to give it to someone."[12] Numerous conversations and formal interviews clearly revealed that Sea Grant officials were not inclined to promote the use of TEDS. Furthermore, considerable doubt over NMFS's claims for TEDS existed within the Sea Grant community over the soundness of the scientific data on which NMFS based its claims for TEDS. In fact, the reason the Academy of Sciences reported doubt over government's claims about TEDS is because of the testimony of Sea Grant gear experts. We interviewed the same gear experts the Academy did. The majority of marine agents (not just gear experts or just Louisiana agents) were not convinced of either the necessity or the efficacy of the NMFS TED.

It is possible that a number of agents worked to get other type TEDS certified precisely because they saw the futility in trying to get shrimpers to adopt what they themselves had little faith in. Whether or not this is a proper inference is arguable. What is clear is that marine agents had serious misgivings about the NMFS TED. In the words of a gear expert: "They were ready to blockade the harbors, but I convinced them not to. Not that I'm for TEDS, I'm not. They finally had a good attitude about using them, and I felt that I didn't want to ruin that."[13] Another gear expert added: "In 1986 [and 19]87, all there was was the NMFS big TED. I had problems [with it]. It takes rocket science to get it to work. They came out with a mini-TED. It fished the same."[14] Of course some marine agents were upset with shrimpers for not trying the TEDS: "A lot of shrimpers spent this time [during the voluntary period] bucking the TEDs. They should have been learning how to use them. They don't know how they work. In some bottoms the TEDs collapse if you don't rig them right. The productivity is way down."[15] But one marine agent explained why many shrimpers were against even trying TEDs; and in the process of explaining the shrimpers' attitude reveals his own: "They [shrimpers] developed a cannonball-shooter to avoid the jellyfish, which are like large hard balls. They only used it [the shooter] when the shrimp concentrated in the sea of jellyfish. If the amount of shrimp loss was high, they simply stopped shrimping. In other words, from the beginning of TEDs, [shrimpers] knew that these devices lose shrimp. Anyone who said otherwise they presumed was lying."[16] Early interviews yielded guarded responses, but later, as agents became more familiar with us, their remarks became more frank and not one we interviewed could be described as sanguine about the NMFS TED.

Understandably, NMFS officials perceived a different situation from Sea Grant. Andy Kemmerer, director of NMFS's Southeast office, responded:

> [Sea Grant] Extension was created to replace the NMFS's advisory mission which existed prior to 1970. With the creation of Sea Grant in 1970, there was an adjustment of missions. NMFS got rid of its advisory service. Sea Grant was to take NMFS's research [on fishing and shrimping gear] and transfer it. . . . Prior to implementation [of TEDs], our relationship with Sea Grant on TED issues was excellent. Once the regulations went into effect, however, the relationship became very strained. . . . Our initial assumption with TEDs was that Sea Grant would take information we provided and transfer it to the shrimping industry. This did not always work. In some instances, some Sea Grant agents were publicly critical. . . . We entered the period of "this TED is better than the NMFS TED." And, at times we were portrayed as trying to force the NMFS TED down the throat of the industry. Seldom did we ever hear that NMFS was funding research by Sea Grant to investigate other TED designs. Indeed, we funded virtually all the research that went on with TEDs. . . . Our goal was to identify as many alternatives to the NMFS TED as possible. . . . We tried our best to avoid arguments of which TED was best by establishing a policy to stay out of such public debates. This was tough to do because we were being falsely identified by some in the media and by industry as the "bad guys" who were trying to force every shrimper to pull a NMFS TED. . . . There were enough cool heads on both sides [NMFS and Sea Grant] to repair damage [tension] when it occurred. I think we are now back to where we were before [TEDs]. Fences have been mended, although a few scars may still exist.[17]

Obviously, both agencies recognized the tension caused by TEDs, although each agency attributed different causes. Was NMFS so committed to TEDs that it was asking Sea Grant to be an enforcer? Were Sea Grant agents simply unwilling to acknowledge the help NMFS was delivering to shrimpers through its gear research? Certainly, during the TEDS conflict NOAA conducted workshops to work out differences between NMFS and Sea Grant that the TEDS conflict uncovered. One workshop directed all parties to say nothing disparaging of TEDS publicly. This move clearly indicates the seriousness of the tension, but it was only one of the contextual problems exacerbating the TEDS conflict.

MEDIATION: THE AGREEMENT THAT SLPPED AWAY

TSA requested mediation from NOAA when both the shrimping industry and environmentalists were unwilling to accept the government's plan. Briefly, the plan involved requiring TEDS only when concentrations of turtles warranted it. The plan would have mandated TEDS only in specific areas and times of the year. The plan was unacceptable to both parties in the conflict, but both sides did agree to negotiate. The drama of TEDS continued to be played out during negotiations. NOAA provided the arrangements and selected the participants.

Four mediation meetings were held in 1986—in New Orleans; Jekyll Island, Georgia; Houston; and Washington, D.C. A mediation team headed by a government-appointed arbitrator, Larry Cotter, was assembled. Although the results of the mediation are well known, the process has not previously been investigated. Initial accord and near agreement evaporated when the president of Concerned Shrimpers, Tee John Mialjevich, refused to sign the arbitration agreement. Subsequently, TSA repudiated the agreement signed by their representative at the meetings.

The mediation team that met at New Orleans in October, 1986, was composed of twelve members, six on the environmentalists' side and six on the industry side. Two lawyers for the Center for Marine Conservation, along with Michael Weber, who headed the turtle initiative for the Center, together with representatives from Greenpeace, Environmental Defense Fund, and Monitor International, made up the environmental side. On the industry side, the Southeast Fisheries Association lawyer, Elton Greenberg; Clinton Willis of the Cataret Boatman's Association of South Carolina; Charles Lyles of Louisiana Shrimp Association; David Eymard of the Texas Shrimp Association; Leonard Crosby, Jr., of the Bryan County Georgia Co-Op; and Tee John Mialjevich represented the industry at the negotiations. Only two members of the mediation team, Leonard Crosby, Jr., and Tee John, made their living trawling for shrimp. Through four often-heated meetings, the participants argued and negotiated their respective positions.

In examining the mediation process, we relied on documentary evidence, including the agreement documents and observers' notes. We also interviewed the

parties and used these interviews to reconstruct the subjective events as participants saw them.

Consistent with the dramatic character of the TEDS conflict, negotiations evoked
a complex constellation of emotions. High hopes and jubilation over a near-agree-
ment was followed by surprise, dismay, and helplessness as the would-be agreement evaporated.

SELECTION PROCESS

In selecting representation from the shrimping industry, NOAA did not consult
with NMFS officials who had actually worked with industry. Instead, NOAA administrator Anthony Calio relied on Ralph Rayburn, a personal friend, for advice. As
the executive director of the Texas Shrimp Association, Rayburn played a large
role in selecting representatives on the industry side. His belief that shrimpers had
to adopt TEDS or face closure influenced his suggestions to Calio:

> Calio called me to see if we [five or six representatives of the industry] would meet
> in Washington very quickly. Calio said that he would propose to close shrimping in
> turtle "hot spots" and would draw the line on the map, but I said that environ-
> mentalists would tear it apart. Jack Brauner [former director of the NMFS southeast
> office) said, "Let's propose a tighter plan. Calio thought this may be better and sent
> us a letter proposing to delay [the] plan if we would agree to federal mediation. . . .
> [The] negotiating team was limited to five people [on the shrimp industry side],
> but Tee John was invited to be on the panel. . . . The [endangered Kemp's] ridley sea
> turtles were the principal concern. [The other four species are classified as threatened;
> ridleys feed in shallow waters.] We were looking at ten fathoms. . . . Tee John said,
> "If you close out to ten fathoms, you might as well close out to two hundred miles"
> [i.e., close shrimping in U.S. waters]. We could have gotten the ten fathom line.
> [That is, Rayburn is saying that were it not for Tee John, shrimpers trawling beyond
> the ten-fathom line would not be required to use TEDS. Since trawling off the coast
> of Texas is done in deep water, TEDS would not be required.]. . . . Tee John led us to
> believe that he would sign [by the fourth and final meeting held in Washington,
> D.C., but then] his mother died.[18]

Tee John left the meeting and subsequently returned, but he refused to sign. Shortly
thereafter, the Texas Shrimp Association's board members repudiated their
representative's decision to sign. Rayburn assessed the situation this way:

> [Tee John] didn't sign because he saw he could make a living off this [situation] for
> four to five years. . . . The meetings were tense and hard. Industry [as opposed to
> industry leaders] did not realize how severe the impact would be if settlement was

not made. We [industry representatives] did know how serious [the impact would be].... Things I was most concerned with were the possibility of closing shrimping and the effect on the industry, [also] the possibility of boycotting, which would have a devastating effect on the market. I was surprised that they [environmentalists] hadn't [boycotted]. Although, Audubon did briefly talk about it, but it didn't go anywhere. They didn't have [the] heart for it. [They] wanted to focus on the shrimpers who were destructive. [Rayburn mentioned the outspoken shrimpers of Louisiana.] But [Audubon and other environmental groups] didn't want to hurt positive shrimpers and couldn't come up with a workable plan.[19]

Rayburn's comments reflect many dimensions of the TEDS conflict in general and TEDS mediation in particular. To begin with, a division existed in the industry between owner operators (shrimpers who shrimp for a living) and fleet owners who hire vessel captains and crew. The Texas Shrimp Association reflected both interests but leaned toward the latter. Thus, Rayburn was aware that Tee John's appeal was to a different segment of the industry. According to Rayburn, both Rayburn and Calio reluctantly added Tee John on the industry side. The dynamic operating was that both the Texas Shrimp Association and the government were forced to reckon with the grassroots challenge to business as usual. As with other government agencies, the natural tendency was for the Department of Commerce to rely on established relationships to implement new regulations. Industry's access to government was now being challenged by both the environmentalists and a grassroots movement of independent owner-operators. Rayburn assisted the government in choosing the representatives on the industry side. Kemmerer, the present director of NMFS Southeast office, argued that this task should have been given to people in government, namely, NMFS, who had worked closely with industry.[20] But Calio sidelined the NMFS officials. Despite internal objections to the process, the "good ol' boy" pattern was followed. But the established ways of doing business with the shrimp industry was changing because NOAA could no longer maintain autonomy from the goals of both the environmental movement and the grassroots movement of shrimpers. The end result, for structuring representation, was that a rather loose geographical principle was applied.

Inevitably, questions about representation were raised. North Carolina threatened to file a lawsuit. Divisions arose between those who shrimped for a living and those who did not. Processors and packers who had been increasingly benefiting from cheaper imported shrimp did not have much at stake. The fundamental error made by government in selecting the industry side was not giving enough attention to the representation. Even when organizations are represented by their leaders, members will abrogate their leaders when leaders fail to respect the wishes of members. This is what happened in the case of the Texas Shrimp Association. Former vice president of CSA and present TSA Board member, Wilma Anderson, commented:

> I questioned Ralph on this [issue of representation]. He said, "We got to limit our losses." He persuaded TSA to go to the mediation. We went to New Orleans. David Eymard and three other TSA board members who just came on were there. Ralph told me he couldn't poll all the board members. Eymard was chosen [by Ralph and the on-the-spot poll] to represent TSA. Ralph made the phone calls to poll members. . . . In D.C., . . . Calio walked in; someone asked three of us to leave, since we were not part of the mediation team. Calio let me stay. [Anderson and Calio were old acquaintances.] Calio walked over to Eymard and told him how proud he was of Eymard's dad. Calio then tells the group they would be pulling TEDs twelve months out of the year if they don't come to some agreement with environmentalists. After this meeting, Calio asked me what I thought. [Calio said,] "I'll see that Texas shrimpers don't pull TEDs." [Calio was presumably counting on an agreement that would not require TEDs in deep water, since Texas shrimp are caught in deep water.] . . . The mediation agreement came out, but the TSA Board did not vote on it. David Cottingham [of the Office of Chief Scientist, NOAA] called me and asked, "What is the Board going to do?" Julius Collins [then-chairman of the Gulf Council] called and told me Eymard signed it. We went through hell getting TSA's name off that. We had to settle for some lines in the Congressional records.[21]

Other Board members have confirmed that their representative, Eymard, while duly commissioned to represent the membership, was specifically told not to sign any document without the vote of board members, as required by the bylaws of TSA. The Board members we have interviewed also share Anderson's opinion of Rayburn's role in the negotiation meetings:

> He [Rayburn] was so involved [with] other issues, such as energy use in the Gulf, that he did not represent shrimper interests in the TEDs negotiations. I quit being involved with his [TSA] group. (Some members quit TSA after the ill-fated negotiations and joined Concerned Shrimpers). He was an Extension agent [before being hired as executive director of TSA. He also worked on a Ph.D. at Texas A&M but never got his degree]. Rayburn is not even from Texas and knows little about commercial fishing. He is good friends with Walter Fondren [son of the founder of Humble Oil; he founded GCCA and served as chairman of the Gulf Council].[22]

Thus, the Texas Shrimp Association repudiated the agreement. Signatories from the Atlantic Coast were not representing any organization. They were there to give geographical representation in the broadest sense of the term. The sole lawyer on the industry side did represent Florida's commercial shrimpers inasmuch as some of the Southeast Fisheries Association membership includes shrimpers. The Louisiana shrimper present, Tee John Mialjevich, did represent a significant number of independent shrimpers of the Gulf and South Atlantic, particularly in his home state of Louisiana. Even so, there were a number of other associations in Louisiana and far more nonmembers than members of Concerned Shrimpers. At the height of its popularity among shrimpers, CSA could not have had more than 10 percent of all shrimpers enrolled.

LIMITATIONS TO NEGOTIATING

Apart from the problems of representation, the most significant impediment to genuine negotiation appears to have been the belief among most signatories on the industry side that they were not at liberty to create a more favorable-to-industry agreement. This attitude was, at least in part, the result of the interpersonal style with which administrator Calio directed the meetings. On more than one occasion in private, Calio stressed that shrimpers would face grave consequences if they could not strike an agreement with environmentalists. Having questioned signatories and one Sea Grant marine agent who was privy to these conversations, we can understand how one could interpret Calio's words as a threat. Accordingly, some signatories on the shrimpers' side felt that genuine negotiations were out of reach and, therefore, any negotiation was better than a closed fishery or TEDs twelve months of the year in all waters. According to Leonard Crosby, Georgia shrimper and signatory to the agreement: "Calio took us in a private room and closed the doors. He said, 'Don't let anything we say leave this room.' He told us we had to stay with the environmentalists until we had an agreement. He said, 'If you don't come out with an agreement, you'll be pulling TEDs for 365 days of the year.' Yeah, I signed. With the agreement we had to pull TEDs for only four months. But last week the Georgia Commission passed the ruling [requiring that] we got to pull TEDs from April to December. The agreement didn't do us any good."[23]

Since 1990 the latest TEDs regulations mandate TEDs be used twelve months of the year, precisely what Crosby thought he was avoiding.

Other signatories and observers of the TEDs agreement on the shrimpers' side recounted the events similarly. Eyewitnesses at the last mediation session held in Washington, D.C., suggested that Calio's actions fell just inside the line that separates firmness from intimidation.

A REASONABLE SOLUTION IS REJECTED

Turtles are not equally encountered in all locations, depths, and seasons. Mandating TEDs only when turtles are likely to be present would appear to be a reasonable solution. But both environmentalists and shrimpers rejected this approach. The final TEDs regulations promulgated were less than reasonable according to a number of government people in both NMFS and Sea Grant Extension Service. In brief, their collective expectation was that a regulation more sensitive to turtle concentrations would emerge from the agreement. Weber expected the same thing:

> We were not going to get what we wanted—all waters all times. Nonetheless, . . . we [environmentalists] agreed to focus on areas we all [parties] agreed would be "hot spots". Basically, [we] hammered out what we regarded as an interim agreement that would phase in TEDs. . . . Far less than what we [hoped] to get out of the process. We were trying to be careful so as not to be undercutting the benefits. We bought into the general principle of "hot spots". Tried to build in some performance standards [The idea was to get the shrimpers to voluntarily use TEDs so that there would be no need for mandating TEDs.]. . . . On the last evening, Tee John didn't think he could sell it [interim plan] to the shrimpers. Folks on our side tried to come up with a solution. . . . It didn't sit well. Others in industry [TSA] signed off. We were willing to accept [for several years] a level of TEDs use that required the least amount of [TED effort]. Everything came unglued and the agreement was challenged. The offshore shrimpers wanted to include TEDs in all inshore waters at all times. [Some offshore shrimpers] were willing to [hurt] the inshore fishermen.[24]

Perhaps the president of Concerned Shrimpers inclined toward an across-the-board regulation that would impact all shrimpers alike. At the time, many participants considered this position unnecessary and may have helped shift the regulation toward the unreasonable side. Tee John's motivations were based on the possible danger that shrimpers would be divided and, therefore, more easily manipulated. But his critics reported to us that his actions were an attempt to broaden the conflict and extend the power base of Concerned Shrimpers. Whatever motivation lay behind the insistence on an across-the-board regulation, the TEDs drama was developing in ways that few in government wanted or anticipated. The representation problems and the impediments to true negotiations were not the only dynamic affecting the scenes.

Several informants provided leads indicating that ChemWaste funded the Center for Environmental Education's fight to protect turtles. These same informants also insisted that the TEDs conflict was a continuation of other conflicts that first began in the regional Fisheries and Management Councils.

THE GULF COUNCIL AND THE
SOUTH ATLANTIC COUNCIL

The Councils make recommendations to the Secretary of Commerce.[25] The South Atlantic Council recommended TEDs to reduce the bycatch of juvenile finfish. By contrast, the Gulf Council avoided the issue.

Before and during the TEDs conflict, an atmosphere of mistrust of the Gulf Council prevailed among fishers. The Gulf Council had earned the reputation, whether deserved or not, of being the most politicized of all of the Councils, possibly, some claimed, because of the political machinations of its former chairmen. Several people, including fishery biologists, referred to a persistent rumor in the Gulf—that a political deal had been struck in the past between shrimpers and a former chairman of the Council, Walter Fondren. Although this issue is addressed in a later chapter, it establishes the bases for mistrust. Despite the efforts of able and dedicated staffers to counter this rumor and other similar ones, the Gulf Council was hard-pressed to establish full trust among fishers.

To date, the Gulf Council still makes recommendations on the shrimp fishery, but it steered away from the TEDs issue before final issuance of TEDs regulations in 1989. Although TEDs were discussed at Gulf Council meetings, no formal recommendations on TEDs were made to the Secretary of Commerce. To explain the situation, some members of the Gulf Council privately commented that no one wanted to take on shrimping, the largest and most powerful fishery. If not, then why did the South Atlantic Council encourage TEDs? Fish and Wildlife pushed for protection of sea turtles more aggressively than did NMFS. They successfully joined forces with environmental groups to influence the South Atlantic Council's pro-TEDs decision. An examination of the role government assumed may explain why the Gulf Council and the South Atlantic Council had different positions on TEDs.

GOVERNMENT IS A PLAYING FIELD

Movement and countermovement try to influence government policy in a variety of ways. Some agencies and structures are more insulated than others. Established relationships with powerful groups act as barriers to the penetration by new groups. An example will clarify our point.

In her analysis of the civil rights movement, sociologist Jill Quadagno argues that the Labor Department had established ties with trade unions.[26] The Labor Department was less aggressive in pursuing civil rights issues than the Justice Department, which was more insulated from the influence of trade unions. Obviously, the reverse is also true. The Justice Department was structurally insulated from trade unions, but civil rights groups had access to it. The parallel in the TEDS case is striking. The Department of Commerce and its subsidiary agencies (NOAA, NMFS, Sea Grant), as well as the management councils, had established close ties with the user groups they advise and regulate. One should expect federal agencies that do not have established ties with commercial harvesters to be more insulated and, therefore, more aggressive in implementing new regulations. Fish and Wildlife Service became to the environmental movement what the Justice Department had been to the civil rights movement.

The ties that commercial harvesters have enjoyed with various agencies of the Department of Commerce has been a counterforce to the environmental groups. Now, however, new alignments between these agencies and commercial harvesters are being formed. There is every reason to expect considerable variation in the rate at which environmental interests penetrate the agencies of the Department of Commerce. As environmental groups gain access to the respective agencies of the Department of Commerce, business will no longer be as usual. Understandably, agencies serving weak and splintered commercial interests have penetrated the quickest. One could also argue that, all other things being equal, new alignments will also emerge more quickly in NMFS than in Sea Grant.[27] One reason is that Sea Grant is structurally more insulated from national environmental groups inasmuch as state structures overlay the federal organization of Sea Grant. Second, Sea Grant serves a single client, commercial harvesters. Unlike NMFS, it has no charge to protect marine species nor does it play an enforcement role. However, since Sea Grant has state level connections, it must come to grips with the extent to which environmental groups penetrate, not only the Department of Commerce, but also respective state agencies. Accordingly, there may develop more influence on Sea Grant by environmental groups in Georgia and Florida than in Louisiana. A similar argument can be made to explain the divergence on TEDS between the Gulf Council and the South Atlantic Council.

Although the "state is the playing-field on which the never-ending battle between movement and countermovement forces is fought,"[28] the state is not a neutral bystander to resource conflicts.[29] It is not a disinterested party, but neither is it the obedient servant of the powerful. The state and state agencies have their own interests to serve, and they often have both public and private agendas that influence and are influenced by the private sector. Because government is not monolithic, different levels and agencies may pursue different goals. The result is that social movements can change government, but government may also exert considerable influence over the path and rate of change.

The TEDS conflict was not limited to user groups or confined between shrimpers and federal regulatory agencies. The controversy enveloped relations between the states and the federal government and between branches and agencies of the federal government. The TEDS conflict has had a significant impact on government and has been a contributing cause to changes in government agencies. Whether for or against TEDS, every government agency entering the fray used science to promote its position. But science itself was enveloped by the conflict, and truth, based on science, became one of the first casualties of the TEDS conflict. The impact that the TEDS controversy had on science is the next part of the drama.

Chapter

5

Science and Magic

Early in our research, we encountered a variety of opinions about how science is used in fisheries management. This chapter examines the gap between what contenders expected from science and what they received. It is about how those expectations tempted scientists to perform magic.

Science is a product of a community of men and women who are as subject to social influences and individual shortcomings as other men and women. Likewise, ideas and practices go in and out of style in the scientific community.[1] The coming and going of ideas, theories, and techniques is not always perfectly correlated with the progress of science. Indeed, fads, fashions, and foibles are as common in scientific communities as they are in societies.[2] An example might be helpful.

Attitudes changed in the medical community concerning the dangers of childbirth past the age of thirty. One may wonder if the change in attitude is solely the result of new evidence or new social attitudes and arrangements. Perhaps the change came in response to the desire of greater numbers of women in their thirties to have their first child?

But scientists do not adopt a new opinion without cause. Ritual is used to construct a new reality, which usually means presenting new evidence. But it can also mean a new interpretation of existing evidence. In many cases, it involves a formal or informal vote of scientists, as was the case when the Academy of Sciences published its report on turtle mortality. A ritual transformation of reality takes place. The new opinion is more convincing when numbers are imposed.

The magical properties attributed to numbers dates to antiquity. Pythagoras saw in numbers a spiritual power that contemporary science has rejected. Yet magic and ritual have always been important dimensions in social life and what was thrown out has reentered under a different guise. Numbers bestow a factuality that is difficult to produce any other way. They disguise uncertainty, and their appeal is strong in cultures that have legitimated science as the sole arbiter of truth. It is primarily through the use of numerical extrapolations and population simulations that the ritual dimension of science can best be illustrated in the TEDS conflict.

The original government study estimated that 30,000 sea turtles were caught and killed each year by trawls.[3] The National Academy of Sciences reviewed this and other studies and concluded that 50,000 was a better estimate.[4] In both instances, the number of actual turtles caught in shrimp trawls was extrapolated. Actual numbers of turtles caught were multiplied by shrimping effort (number of trawls, number of tows per trip, the duration of tows, and the number of trips). The resulting extrapolated number represents the number of turtles caught in trawls in a single year for a specific zone of the Gulf or South Atlantic. The estimates of each zone were then summed to get the total turtles caught for the entire waters of the Gulf and South Atlantic. Each figure used to derive the estimated total turtles caught was itself an estimate. Obviously, the total estimate is only as accurate as the specific estimates from which it was derived. Unfortunately, in extrapolations errors, such as overestimates or underestimates, are multiplied.

Similarly, population simulation presents a temptation to commit ritual. Based on population dynamics, mathematical models can be used to estimate the total number of organisms in a given environment. By knowing the fertility rates of age classes (number of organisms under one year old, one to two years old etc.), mortality rates, and the distribution of age classes, changes in the population (expanding, stable, or declining) can be predicted. As in the case of extrapolation, errors in estimating are multiplied by the mathematics employed.

Fishery plans are driven by estimates of marine stocks calculated by mathematical models similar to the technique used to study human populations. Reliance on mathematical modeling has increased, in part because computers can perform complex calculations more quickly. Consequently, modeling has become a useful tool in assessing marine stocks. Nonetheless, there is still a considerable amount of uncertainty attached to modeling, but this problem is partially hidden because the predictions are expressed numerically. It is not wholly the scientist's fault if policymakers and the public endow numbers with more certainty than they possess. Often rushed to give speedy and decisive answers to predictions that are tentative, fishery scientists made declarations that had as much affinity to magic and ritual as they had to science. A stock may be overfished, underutilized, or recovering, as the case may be. The complexity of nature is dismissed by the demands of policy. These facts do not question the legitimacy of modern fishery science, but call attention to the difference between the ideal of science and the actual scientific process as it comes under the influence of social processes. The goal of science to know for knowledge's sake is abandoned as other demands are made of science.

In the TEDS case, science functioned to (1) supply information, (2) sustain hopes for vindication or conflict resolution, (3) justify acts, and (4) serve as a weapon in the truth game.

SCIENCE AS INFORMATION

Is the number of turtles declining? What is causing the decline? What role does trawling play in that decline? Are TEDS effective in reducing mortality of sea turtles? Do TEDS lose shrimp? These are a few of the questions that science was expected to answer. Although these kinds of questions are routinely addressed by scientists, a gap exists between what answers the parties to the conflict expect and what science can legitimately deliver. Under these conditions, scientists are tempted to act in ways that obscure the differences between social policy and scientific fact.

The National Academy of Sciences was asked to settle the scientific issues associated with TEDS. In early 1990, after some delays, the Academy presented its final report.[5] The Academy requested reviews, and many turtle experts responded to it, including Professor Frank Schwartz of the Institute of Marine Studies at the University of North Carolina at Chapel Hill. Calling attention to statements that the Academy had made with regard to the decline in sea turtle populations, Schwartz said: "Nesting declines, between years, at any one site do not reflect time declines, for many variables affect the observations. See Schwartz (1989) where nesting in one area may be greater or lesser, earlier or later, as a result of environmental or water conditions that are not based or dependent on population levels."[6]

In nine pages of comment to William Fox and Nancy Foster, director and assistant director, respectively, of the National Marine Fisheries Service, Schwartz detailed what he believed were unsubstantiated conclusions drawn by the Academy. He questioned the link between nesting declines and population declines and other major conclusions drawn by the Academy. Schwartz believed that the use of population modeling was unrealistic, that there was no data, and that there was unsubstantial data to support many of the Academy's claims. He also found some of the Academy's data too speculative, and he questioned its dependence on the use of extrapolated data. He succinctly summarized his evaluation: "I thank you for requesting the review. As you can gather, I find the report lacking, full of assumptions, lacking substantiating data, firmly prejudiced that shrimp trawling is the causal agent for sea turtle mortality, and that TEDS are the solution."[7]

Regardless of the Academy's findings or Professor Schwartz's reply, it is important to note the differences in the level of certitude demanded by science on the one hand and policymakers and the general public on the other. Schwartz's comments are illustrative. He repeatedly chided the Academy for making statements that go beyond what the data allow. In effect, he felt that the Academy was making certain what science held either tentatively or for which substantial doubts and uncertainties remain. Scientists hope to discover facts. The public and policymakers want to know the truth, but truth is a certitude. Scientific facts are presented as possible truths, and scientists follow a careful procedure to estimate that probability.[8] Truth is held dogmatically; scientific facts are held tentatively. Scientific facts and theories are always in a state of revision. Thus, a gap in the level of certitude exists between scientific and nonscientific enterprises. This gap fed the fires of controversy in the TEDS case, as Schwartz's letter illustrates. Throughout the TEDS controversy, the effects of this gap were repeatedly noticeable. The differences in the level of certitude may be attributable, not to the level of sophistication of the individuals involved, but to the kind of roles the TEDS parties played. Scientists playing regulatory and policymaking roles impose a different standard than scientists who are playing a research role. Many of the regulators, environmentalists, policymakers, and a few in the shrimping industry were trained in science. However, the demands of their nonscience roles dictated that they push for certainty. A couple of examples help underscore this point.

After the first year of TEDS (compliance was unsatisfactory during the first year of mandated TEDS), nesting counts for Kemp's ridley turtles were up. Environmentalists and some regulators proclaimed, therefore, that TEDS were working. They were certain that (1) the increase in nesting turtles was proof that the population of turtles had increased and (2) that the increase was surely due to TEDS. In a similar way, shrimpers were convinced that TEDS lost shrimp because (1) they personally lost shrimp using TEDS and (2) because others reported losing shrimp using TEDS. No doubts were raised either about the proper rigging of the device nor the accuracy of the reports from others. In both instances certitude replaced the necessary doubt that scientific enterprise requires. By contrast, those scientists not playing advocacy or regulatory roles (for example, Sea Grant scientists connected with universities) appeared much more tentative and cautious.

The uncertainties that science recognizes and the certainty policy and regulation require pose a fundamental dilemma, which involves two equally unsatisfactory errors. Policy and regulations typically utilize uncertain knowledge in choosing between regulating or restricting that which may not need it and failing to restrict or regulate that which requires it. In the first case, society is needlessly expending resources and restricting the use of resources. In the second case, society fails to regulate that which later turns out to be harmful.[9] Ashford (1988) has suggested a general solution to this dilemma that requires an assessment of the risks of committing each type of error. His argument contends that values must guide policymakers and regulators in their decisions.[10] For example, if some doubt exists whether substance x causes cancer, and the costs of regulating substance x is relatively small, policymakers do well to err on the side of caution. Furthermore, the norm of prudence might suggest that even if there is only suspicion that x is carcinogenic, it would be advisable to err on the side of caution. Arguably, Ashford's risk assessment approach is appropriate in the case of hazards and the regulation of alleged toxic substances. Does it, however, have applicability in cases of marine resources? Two different risk scenarios are common in fishery controversies.

Two human use values are involved in the first scenario, and a use value is pitted against the noneconomic value of a species in the second. Routinely, regulators are supplied scientific evidence that harvesting at historical levels will endanger the resource. This judgement is based on some uncertainty. The dilemma they face is clear. In the face of uncertainty, do they impose restrictions on harvesters (short-term loss) in order to maintain a sustainable resource (long-term gain)? If they tarry until all doubt is removed, it may be too late to rescue the resource. Keeping in mind the history of fisheries regulation under the Magnuson Act and the general tendency of user groups to use legitimate doubt to delay regulations, this type of error has been the most frequently committed by managers. Politically, it has been difficult for managers to commit the other type of error. Needlessly restricting the harvest when the resource is in no real danger has not been a commonly committed management error. However, as conservation groups exert more influence, we can expect this error to be more common. But the TEDs conflict does not involve this scenario of risks.

The second scenario, which is relevant in the TEDs case, weighs use value (present harvesting) against the intrinsic value of a species (sea turtles). In this case, two quite different value judgments must be made. Is the gain to turtles significant enough to warrant the loss to shrimpers? Expressed differently, how certain are we over the potential gains and losses? Is regulation warranted if the costs are high and certain and the benefits very small and uncertain? Some would argue that this line of questioning is a moot point because the law (ESA) simply forbids taking of endangered species even if the species' demise is certain under complete protection.

HOPE OF VINDICATION AND CONFLICT RESOLUTION

Throughout our investigation, some TEDs players were hoping scientific facts would vindicate their claims. Still others were hoping that once the whole truth was known, the conflict would be resolved. Here, we examine only the expectations of shrimpers, environmentalists, marine agents, and NMFS officials.

Shrimpers hoped for vindication from the Academy of Science report and from the Office of Management and Budget–mandated study on shrimp loss with TEDS.[11] The Academy upheld the government's contention that trawling endangers turtles but cast doubt on government's claim that TEDS do not lose shrimp. The TEDS Observer Program did report shrimp loss with TEDS but at levels much lower than shrimpers had claimed. Despite these setbacks shrimpers continued to believe that unbiased science would vindicate them. At the November, 1990, meeting of CSA board members, a social scientist reported on his CSA-financed trip in Mexico to Rancho Nuevo, where Kemp ridleys nest, and to Tampico, where the Mexican government was testing TEDS. The presentation, which greatly pleased the Board members, indicated that "the Mexican turtle expert says that pollution is the problem" and that "turtle populations are stable or slightly increasing."[12] What is remarkable about these events is that CSA financed this inquiry when it was experiencing severe financial problems, a fact that underscores the importance shrimpers attached to vindicating evidence. Tee John welcomed more evidence too by encouraging his members to keep records of their catch.

Similarly, other TEDS players looked to science for vindication. Environmentalists found the Academy's report corroborative of their original claim that trawling endangered turtles. Also, environmentalists did not question NMFS reports that claimed no shrimp loss with TEDS. "The government's studies show that TEDS don't lose shrimp", remarked an environmentalist on the TEDS mediation team.[13] Clearly, the speaker was also claiming that environmentalists had been right all along. It was hardly a surprise to anyone when environmentalists produced their own evidence of the wastefulness of trawling. In the summer of 1990 members of the National Audubon Society publicly displayed shrimp trawls overburdened with bycatch of small and unusable finfish. Perhaps the most dramatic event was the interpretation given by a spokesperson of the Audubon Society when a small increase in the number of nesting Kemp ridleys was reported in 1991. The spokesperson contended that after two years of TEDS use, nesting had increased, meaning, of course, that their effort was not for naught.[14] But government too needed vindication, and, like shrimpers and environmentalists, they looked to science for it.

Marine agents wanted the conflict behind them. Although some agents made unfavorable public statements about TEDS and the majority remained unconvinced of their efficacy, most wanted the conflict resolved. When one agent tried to tell a group of shrimpers that the shrimpers could not stop TEDS, "I had problems, I damn near got thrown off the dock. They didn't like the message I was bringing".[15] One agent worked extensively to get non-NMFS TEDS certified (approved by NMFS) and to convince the Georgia shrimpers that compliance was in their best interest.[16] Agents were hoping that shrimpers would learn to use TEDs and reduce their shrimp loss. In effect, they were hoping that shrimpers would generate their own scientific evidence—perhaps not in favor of TEDs but favorable enough that they could at least live with the device. In contrast to marine agents, NMFS officials not only wanted a resolution of the bitter controversy, they also needed vindication of their role in TEDs.

NMFS officials wanted to avoid conflict from the very beginning. No doubt, NMFS officials had different motivations among them, but collectively NMFS wished to head off conflict. On numerous occasions, officials indicated that they were unwilling to alienate the shrimping industry. Ironically, the path NMFS took to mitigate conflict—by using TEDs, a technical solution—plummeted the agency into a tête-à-tête with shrimpers. NMFS tried to push the use of TEDs to prevent a long and protracted legal battle with environmentalists, but in doing so, it asked science to vindicate an agency action. The NMFS southeast region director claimed: "When used properly, TEDs exclude turtles, and our data shows a 2 percent increase in catch [of shrimp], but we didn't think that was significant, so we reported no difference in catch. Now some [environmentalists] have come along and have made the claim [that] it catches more shrimp. But, we didn't think we should make that claim, although our data shows about a 2 percent higher catch with TEDs."[17]

NMFS was sold on TEDs because they sought and found supporting evidence. But vindication of a policy or regulation is not a legitimate role of science. If one sets out to prove or disprove that TEDs work, both goals are identically biased. And both are very different from setting out to examine evidence for and against the device. Once NMFS had committed itself to vindicating an action, it could no longer protect the legitimacy of its scientific products. This is so because (1) objectivity is compromised inside the agency when the agency's bias is communicated to in-house scientists, and (2) outside the agency, potential consumers lose faith in the objectivity of both the scientific work done inside the agency and research conducted under its auspices. Not surprisingly, NMFS was fearful of evidence outside of its sphere of influence. An unpublished pilot study of TEDs done by Louisiana Sea Grant staff cast doubt on the effectiveness of the NMFS TED. The principal investigator of that study guardedly recalled the events:

> For several years . . . I was very much involved on the TEDs issue and was interested in seeing a settlement reached. . . . I was hoping to see the issue resolved, and we [Louisiana Sea Grant] proposed this study of TEDs. We worked up a good statistical model that would do a dual comparison of TEDs versus no TEDs on the trawler that would account for causes in any variable conditions that might arise. We were opti-

mistic that something could be achieved by this type of study. We believed that the
TEDS technology was developed to allow us to compare several types of TEDS to find
one that would be most suitable for our conditions [in Louisiana coastal waters]
. . . . [We were] optimistic that we would get something [e.g., funding for the pro-
posal]. We were surprised when Andy Kemmerer [NMFS director of the southeast
region] told us that the TEDS technology had not been developed sufficiently for the
type of study we were proposing. I also got a feeling—nothing concrete, just a feeling—that the environmental representatives did not believe that we at LSU were
really interested in a serious study of TEDS. We did do [a] limited study. . . . However, we were hoping to be able to do more.[18]

Eventually, NMFS did certify other TEDS but only after a number of very dedicated Sea Grant Extension Service gear specialists worked tirelessly testing and
retesting other, more shrimper-friendly teds. It is interesting to note here that it
was a shrimper-developed device, modified by gear experts, that has proven to be
the most effective in reducing shrimp loss.[19]

SCIENCE AS JUSTIFICATION

There is a distinction between vindication and justification. An agency is vindi-
cated when its position on an issue is subsequently supported by science. It is justified when its original position is proven right. Vindication has public relations
dimensions, but its focus is internal. In vindication the agency is consoled that
the position taken is supported by science and that its competency has been upheld. It has done a good job and can dismiss self-doubts about its ability and judgment. On the other hand, justification is outward-looking when science is used to
legitimate actions and to establish the truth (socially constructed reality) that others
must assent to because that truth is undeniable. In vindication the internal doubts
are dismissed. In justification objective reality has been socially created. Empiri-
cally, it is difficult to separate the two for they are typically interwoven. Agencies
typically desire that their position be the correct one and that others accept that
position as the truth. However, there are instances in which an agency is not interested in whether facts are true or not, but simply desires to foster its version of the
truth. Under those circumstances, one finds unabashed manipulation of facts for
public consumption. Before one concludes that the Coast Guard put a spin on
compliance, the evidence must be weighed carefully.

During the post-blockade period of 1990, shrimpers, particularly in the central Gulf, continued to resist TEDS. Based on estimates given by shrimpers, marine
agents, and others familiar with the industry, compliance in the central Gulf could
not have been much higher than 40 to 50 percent. Such estimates were easy to

obtain since anyone driving past the docks could see from a distance whether nets were rigged with TEDs. Based on Coast Guard statistics, NMFS officials reported compliance levels of over 90 percent at a time when CSA was still telling shrimpers that TEDs violations drew only civil penalties and that shrimpers could refuse to pay the fines. Many shrimpers in the central Gulf did not hide their noncompliance.

Environmentalists were also concerned about low compliance, so they requested compliance data from the Coast Guard, although they believed the Coast Guard was not vigorously enforcing TEDs use.[20]

In the summer of 1990 NMFS officials decided to impose criminal penalties on violators of TEDs regulations. The chief enforcement officers of the southeast region office of NMFS explained the motivation behind the action: "NMFS plays a primary role in training C[oast] G[uard] and responsibility for cases. This year [1990] has been different in that in July we [NMFS] went criminal." Thus, NMFS was powerless to force payment in the civil cases since property could not be seized. The process was a kind of game shrimpers played with NMFS. The NMFS official continued: "We [NMFS and the shrimping leaders, typically TSA] get together whenever we have a change in policy. We met with the industry in Houston and told them we are going criminal. We are not playing."[21] The new regulations now meant that shrimpers' catch and vessels could be legally seized.

We inferred that compliance could not have been as high as 90 percent in 1990. Instead, we concluded that the Coast Guard compliance data in 1990 was not accurate. Furthermore, a Coast Guard officer told us that the compliance data was massaged for public consumption. The informant claimed that his duties included working with TEDs boarding statistics.

If the Coast Guard actually put a spin on compliance data, it certainly would not be the first time a government agency did so. If data were actually manipulated, perhaps the Coast Guard was justifying itself. In justification, when the evidence points to a wrong conclusion, the agency merely creates facts to demonstrate that it has effectively and vigorously performed its duties. But constructing reality is the same as lying. If the Coast Guard played with numbers, what was their motivation—to increase compliance by convincing noncomplying shrimpers they are in the minority, a strategy to stave off environmentalists, a disguise for its lack of resources to enforce regulations? Or was the Coast Guard getting even with shrimpers who embarrassed them during the blockade? All speculations, of course, but contenders on both sides of the TEDs conflict hurled such charges. When science becomes a weapon in group conflict, objectivity is irretrievably lost.

SCIENCE AS A WEAPON IN GROUP CONFLICT

A weapon is any device or method used in fighting to harm, diminish, or vanquish one's opponent. Throughout the TEDS conflict, shrimpers and environmentalists used science as a weapon. Environmentalists used turtle strandings to sound the charge against shrimpers. The stranding data were examined by the National Academy of Sciences, which projected even higher levels of turtle mortality than previously published government reports. The report was a powerful weapon for environmentalists. It corroborated the most important charge they made against trawling—namely, that trawling endangers sea turtles. The Academy's report cast doubt on the claims made by environmentalists and NMFS that TEDS did not lose shrimp. But the Academy's facts—that 50,000 turtles are killed annually by trawling—were used by environmentalists in their war on trawling. Science had become an offensive weapon in the war over marine resources. Similarly, shrimpers also used science as a weapon but largely for defensive purposes, as they did with the findings of the TEDS Observer Program.

Although the TEDS Observer Program provided evidence that TEDS lose shrimp, it also recorded the number of turtles caught. When no turtles were reported caught in Texas waters by the shrimpers participating in the program, shrimpers used the evidence to defend their position that shrimping did not endanger turtles in certain areas and at certain depths. They used this information to cast doubt on the evidence that trawling endangers sea turtles.

But environmentalists and shrimpers were not alone in using science as a weapon. During the TEDS conflict, state and federal officials used science as a weapon in battles over turf, resources, and influence as the tension between NMFS and Sea Grant Extension Service illustrates.

TEDS had to be tested in the turtle-rich waters of Cape Canaveral. But since turtles were not even plentiful enough to be caught in a trawl, turtles were actually placed in trawls to speed the testing process. To some gear experts, NMFS officials were more demanding of non-NMFS TEDS than they were of their own device. To some NMFS officials, some Sea Grant marine agents and gear experts were trying to discredit NMFS.

Policy positions tended to direct science rather than science informing policy. On the battlefield of the TEDS conflict, science also became the first casualty. As the standards for judging fact from fiction became compromised, reality itself became elusive.

Chapter

6

The Environmentalists' Challenge

From the beginning of our research, the embedded issues in the TEDS controversy were obvious. One issue involves waste disposal plans for the Gulf of Mexico. This issue surfaced many times during the TEDS conflict, contributing to the intensity of discord and illustrating how environmentalists mobilized to protect endangered and threatened turtles.

THE EMBEDDED ISSUE

Although the Center for Marine Conservation and its former vice president for programs, Michael Weber, were major players in the TEDS controversy, the average shrimper would not be able to identify either the Center or Weber. And, although leaders in the shrimp industry know and like Weber, they do not like the Center and have, in fact, often challenged the legitimacy of the Center's motives to save the turtle. Their charge is that Waste Management Incorporated contributed money to the Center for Marine Conservation, the organization that played the lead role in pushing TEDS. Waste Management Incorporated paid $45,000 to an environmental lawyer, one of the most knowledgeable lawyers on fishery issues in Washington, D.C., to help the environmentalists at the negotiation sessions. Waste Management also funded the Center for Marine Conservation during a financial crisis. Industry leaders believe Waste Management's motivation to help environmentalists was to get even with shrimpers for protesting against waste disposal in the Gulf. With the shrimpers out of the way, the company could resume its plans for waste disposal.[1] Were it not for Waste Management's assistance, the environ-mentalists would have had to have settled for less at the negotiations. According to a TSA board member, "If there had been no third-party interests [waste disposal] present, TEDs would have been mandated for certain times and places. The deep-water Texas shrimping grounds [where turtles are seldom encountered] would not have been included."[2]

At the September, 1990, public meeting of the Gulf Council, which was slated to recommend measures to reduce the bycatch in shrimp trawls, a forceful pre-sentation of a similar charge was delivered by Father Joseph O'Brian of Valley In-terfaith. Father O'Brian was accompanied by at least two busloads of Mexican-American shrimpers from the large deep-water vessels of the lower Texas coast. The group included both crewmen and their wives who had come to speak against the bycatch regulations. Father O'Brian orchestrated these men and women who delivered emotional speeches in both Spanish and English attacking the pend-ing bycatch regulations. Facing his adversaries, Father O'Brian addressed the Coun-cil. Supported by pamphlets depicting Dean Buntrock, CEO of Waste Management, as an octopus whose tentacles reached far into environmental organizations and government agencies, he expounded in detail on Waste Management Incorporated's role in the TEDS regulations. He fixed his gaze on Council Chairman Walter Fondren, Jr., and accused him of knowledge of and duplicity in these evil minis-trations.[3] The episode visibly shook Fondren as well as others on the Council. The Council decided to postpone bycatch reduction plans.

When we questioned Michael Weber on these charges, his response was, "It is difficult for me to find adequate language to express the outrageousness of the charge."[4] Weber explained that a good argument could be constructed for envi-ronmental groups accepting money from corporations. He stressed the need for "clearly stated policies and principles. . . . It should not be left up to the CEO."

One of the private attorneys for the environmentalists gave a similar response: "Two women [Wilma Anderson and Deyaun Boudreaux, TSA board members] are spreading the word among shrimpers through newsletters that ChemWaste [subsidiary of Waste Management Incorporated] has a conspiracy against them. The fact is that the attorneys are well connected with the government bureaucracy and know the ropes and are very knowledgeable about negotiations. ChemWaste is not in the business of poisoning the environment but is in the business of clean-ing up toxic wastes.[5]

Without financial records on corporations, environmental organizations, and individuals, charges made against environmentalists cannot be assessed. But the charges present interesting questions about how sea turtles came to be an impor-tant cause among environmentalists.

PROTECTING TURTLES

The early period of protecting turtles can be divided into two stages—listing and solution finding. Listing endangered species in the 1960s was under the guidelines of the 1966 and 1969 precursors of the Endangered Species Act. By 1970 environmentalists were actively working to protect sea turtles, but in 1973, when the Endangered Species Act was passed, the level of protection increased and extended beyond merely a prohibition of trade in endangered species. In 1975 the Fish and Wildlife Service was petitioned to add three additional species under the protection of the new law. Although the additional listings were legally challenged by the Cayman Turtle Farm, the Environmental Defense Fund successfully fought the challenge in 1977. By 1978 the three species of sea turtles requested in 1975 were included under protection and added to the list of endangered or threatened sea turtles.

From 1977 through 1984 was a period of searching for and refining the most promising solutions. In 1977 environmentalists and representatives of the shrimping industry held a series of meetings at NMFS's southeast region office to discuss possible solutions. The shrimping community preferred a gear modification approach, and the environmentalists concurred. Environmentalists were not happy, however, with the slow pace of NMFS's gear development.

By the late 1970s environmental groups were concerned with turtle protection and the lack of a sense of urgency by NMFS to develop a gear solution. They were alarmed by the turtle strandings in the 1970s and the rapid decrease in the population of Kemp ridleys. Their concern was heightened by data from the Turtle Stranding Network, a network of environmental groups and individuals counting and identifying stranded turtles along the coastline. Established in 1980, the first year of the network's effort suggested a much higher number of stranded sea turtles than had been expected. At about this time, environmentalists met with Dick Frank, NOAA administrator, to get the agency's commitment to intensify gear development. Milton Kaufman of Monitor International, petitioned NMFS to address the problem of turtle strandings. Environmentalists wanted NOAA to design a trawl that would not injure or kill turtles.[6]

That same year the Center for Marine Conservation asked Michael Weber to work on habitat protection. In 1980 he moved from his native California to Washington, D.C., where he was introduced to scientific and conservation literature on the incidental capture of turtles in shrimp trawls.[7] Concomitantly, Weber was involved in the environmentalists' challenge of offshore oil and gas exploration in California. Since environmentalists were successful in stopping offshore oil interests, this success was not only a major victory for the national environmental community but a personally empowering accomplishment for Weber. Thus, he was the logical choice to head the Center's campaign to protect sea turtles.

THE PROCESSES OF MOUNTING A CHALLENGE

The processes of challenging shrimpers (and government, too, for not preventing the incidental capture of turtles by shrimpers) involved choosing a problem, developing a challenge strategy, and mobilizing resources to win.

The environmental movement is embodied in a variety of organizations with different structures, goals, and resources. Concern for the environment finds expression in such organizations as the Sierra Club, Audubon Society, the Center for Marine Conservation, and the Wildlife Fund, among others. In diverse ways and with different resources, each organization defines and pursues its goals.

Goals, tactics, and organizational structure may change as a result of the reception the group receives, and successful groups often change in predictable ways. Often, in the wake of success, what develops is more bureaucracy, a concentration of power at the top, the dilution of original goals, and an abiding concern for organizational survival. A successful organization is one that has been given a place alongside the policymakers and that makes peace with those in power. While the members may still adhere to the more radical, original goals of the organization, they have no power to prevent the leadership from pursuing a different course. To be sure, members can align themselves with other organizations if they wish, but this is a serious threat only to organizations that rely on member support and participation. In the case of the environmental organizations that forced the government to protect turtles, members do not actively participate nor are membership dues the sole means of organizational support. Paid professional staff carry out the policies created by a board of directors. General fund-raising activities (TV, radio, direct mailings) are conducted by marketing firms, and large donations are solicited from corporations. Fundable projects must have mass appeal and corporate support. Saving sympathy-evoking species, such as whales, seals, dolphins, and sea turtles, meets these criteria. Furthermore, more threatening environmental problems (various forms of pollution) may be given less attention by some environmental groups because corporate sponsors would be threatened or public support may not be sustainable. For these reasons, successful national environmental organizations are more likely to choose safe (nonthreatening to corporate America), winnable projects to ensure public sentiment and donations. Thus, as the theory goes, organizational success is followed by a shift in goals. Successful organizations are more likely to have conservative goals and focus on organizational maintenance; existence becomes an end in itself. But perhaps Michael Weber's observation—that it is difficult to say no to money[8]—explains why some environmental groups accept money even from corporations with poor environmental records.

But what benefits do corporations derive from their affiliation with environmental groups? Perhaps corporations are genuinely concerned with environmental issues or they feel responsible to the communities in which they operate. To encourage employees to work for general community improvements is a widely held value in corporate America. But altruistic motives are not wholly inconsistent with profit making.

Few would argue with the claim that corporate image is important for business, and the more tarnished the image, the greater the need to change it. Since it is good public relations to work with environmental groups, many corporations with notorious records as polluters work actively with environmental groups to clean up not only the environment but their images as well.

Some corporations are also anxious to exert some control over the decision-making process of these groups. It would be advantageous for corporations to offer environmental groups guidance in choosing projects. And by doing so, a corporate operation involved in real or potential marine pollution could easily shift attention away from the pollution issue. Coincidentally, environmental groups using their resources to protect turtles could not also combat pollution effectively. Plausible, and, therefore, critics of the close working relationships between some corporations and some environmental organizations are uncomfortable with this arrangement.

DEVELOPING A STRATEGY

Is it better for an environmental group to distance itself from corporate polluters to avoid the temptation to compromise its goals, or is it preferable to work with corporations in the hopes that one can influence the behavior of corporations? The decision whether an environmental organization should seek corporate help can be a serious dilemma. The environmental community itself is divided over this issue. For the most part, the alliance of environmental groups that pushed TEDS worked closely with corporate America and were criticized for it by that segment of the environmental community that sees danger in this approach.

The national environmental community's close working relationship with corporate America has shaped the kind of challenges environmentalists can mount. Consistently, critics of corporate ties with the environmental community have argued that funding is often self-serving. Waste Management Incorporated has profited from tighter restrictions on waste disposal. According to conservative columnist Warren Brookes, "[Waste Management Incorporated] owes most of [its] astonishing rise to something called the Resource Conservation and Recovery Act . . . that is forcing more and more companies to pay huge fees for 'professional' disposal of low-risk waste."[9] Brookes contends that Waste Management Incorporated contributed money to environmental organizations, which, in turn, mounted lawsuits to force stricter standards on waste disposal. The regulated companies and, in some cases, municipal governments, hired Waste Management Incorporated to dispose of their waste. Tighter restrictions and closed municipal landfills were very profitable for Waste Management Incorporated whose profits increased threefold between 1985 and 1990.[10] But the concerns expressed by Brookes are not limited to conservative newspapers. Other newspapers in the country served by the Associated Press have reported similar accounts of the close dealings between corporate polluters and national environmental groups, such as Waste Management's awarding a $40,000 grant in 1990 to the Center for Marine Conservation to fight ocean dumping.[11] The demand for Waste Management's landfills and other land-based operations would eventually increase if dumping in the oceans were curtailed. Waste Management also contributed about $60,000 to the National Audubon Society to support stronger federal regulations of industrial wastes. As Brookes and others argue, the more difficult it becomes for a company to meet environmental regulations, the more it will need Waste Management's services. Waste Management, for its part, pays millions in fines but manages to dispose of the wastes.

Although environmentalists emphasize waste disposal, corporations pay less attention to changing production processes that would reduce the need for disposal. Similarly, the focus on marine debris (garbage from vessels that is thrown overboard) may detract attention from toxic discharges. The reason Waste Management Incorporated contributed to the Center for Marine Conservation's efforts to save endangered turtles lies in the public record of their pattern of funding.

Grassroots environmental groups have warned against the infiltration of the environmental community by corporate polluters. What is most disturbing to the environmental groups who believe environmentalists should distance themselves from corporate polluters is a deepening alliance between corporations with poor environmental records and environmental groups. For example, Philip Rooney, president of Waste Management, is a board member of the National Audubon Society. Dean Buntrock, CEO of Waste Management, is a board member of the National Wildlife Federation. The president of World Wildlife Fund, Kathryn Fuller, sits on the board of Waste Management.[12] William Brown, an executive of Waste Management is on the Board of the Center for Marine Conservation. According to Brian Lipset, Citizens Clearinghouse for Toxic Wastes, the Center for Environmental Education [former name for the Center for Marine Conservation] "had very close connections with Waste Management."[13] Lipset explained how the Center for Marine Conservation and the Society for the Plastics Industry, a proxy group for Brown and Buntrock, worked closely together on marine debris [discarded plastic]. Lipset lists two advantages for corporate presence on boards of environmental groups: corporations can influence the priority of issues and the hiring for key staff positions.[14]

Are these developments the beginning of a new era of cooperation, as the twentieth annual Earth Day proclaimed? Or is it a way for corporations to disarm the opposition to their profitable but ecologically damaging operations? Greenpeace and the National Clearinghouse for Hazardous Wastes are two national grassroots environmental organizations that have publicly attacked the practice.[15]

Understandably, an organization like Greenpeace that refuses corporate funding is critical of environmental organizations that do. However, philosophical differences notwithstanding, Greenpeace had its representative at the TEDs mediation meetings.

The pursuit of the turtle cause by an alliance of corporate-funded environmental organizations did not produce overt conflict or division in the environmental community, at least not among national and international ones. The environmental groups assembled at the mediation meetings gave the appearance that the entire environmental community was behind the effort. Unity was contrived for public and government consumption. However, in reality, local and regional environmental groups, even those affiliated with national groups, did not enthusiastically back the national environmental community's stand on TEDs.[16] A past president of a Sierra Club chapter declared his group's unwillingness to follow the national lead and expressed his suspicion of the national environmental groups' motives.[17] But given the diversity of environmental groups, it is not surprising that the saliency of the turtle issue varied among environmental groups. What is surprising, particularly considering the history of cooperation between commercial fishermen and local environmental groups on marine pollution issues, was the low profile local environmental groups maintained on the TEDs issue. Although one local Audubon Society chapter sought a kinder rapprochement with commercial shrimpers,[18] rumors persisted in the shrimping community that local environmental groups were encouraged to follow the national party line or stay out of the fray.

THE CHALLENGE STRATEGY

Choosing a problem and choosing a strategy to solve the problem are inextricably intertwined.[19] Two aspects of the environmentalists' challenge strategy can help explain why saving turtles became the problem and why the shrimping industry was the target. The first aspect concerned the Endangered Species Act; the second concerned the close ties between the national environmental community and corporate America.

The Endangered Species Act provided the most formidable weapon for concerned citizens to wield at practices that endangered threatened species and their habitat. No actions, whether sponsored by public or private agencies or by government, are immune to the prohibition to refrain from endangering species or critical habitat. Under provisions of the ESA, any citizen can sue to prevent endangerment. Furthermore, the act mandates that government agencies, chiefly, the Fish and Wildlife Service and the National Marine Fisheries Service, publicly list endangered species and plans for recovery. The act has been used to delay undesirable actions by government and private concerns. For example, the Tellico Project was initially blocked because it threatened the habitat of a small endangered fish, the snail-darter. Concern for the spotted owl has temporarily saved old-growth forests in the Northwest. Of course, under provisions of the ESA, threatened and endangered sea turtles mandated shrimpers use TEDs. Understandably, the environmental community has used this most powerful weapon against those they think show disregard for the environment. Accordingly, one can discern an environmental challenge formula. A long-standing pattern of abuse, if left unchecked, will incrementally deplete or destroy a regional, national, or global ecological niche, and little can be done to prevent the abuse precisely because it is incremental. Furthermore, at any one location the degradation may not appear to be serious. Collectively, however, its effects can be disastrous. Given the provisions of ESA, it is good strategy to find a species threatened or endangered by the action, then pursue a legally powerful course of action. When sympathy-evoking species are found, both the law and public sympathy can be mobilized. An obscure plant or animal species is sufficient to mount the legal challenge under ESA. Although environmentalists' concerns are genuine, the endangered species becomes the weapon used to wage war against a more important issue. For example, environmentalists can protect virgin forests precisely because the endangered spotted owl live there. Thus, the presence of the owl gives environmentalists a means to curb the lumber industry. Similarly, damming streams alters the environment, but blocking damming operations is difficult. But, if damming a stream threatens an endangered species, a suit can be filed under the provisions of ESA. Altering the flow patterns of streams was blocked in the Tennessee Valley because the streams were home to an endangered fish, the snail-darter. Similarly, from the environmentalists' point of view, the undesirable practice of trawling in the Gulf and South Atlantic can be curbed because it endangers turtles.

Having selected a problem and a strategy, players must still mobilize resources. To be sure, each process of the environmental challenge in the TEDs case are interrelated. One does not prudently choose a problem that cannot be won, so in making this choice, the organization must evaluate present and potential resources. And it would not be wise to pursue a strategy without assessing one's resources.

MOBILIZING RESOURCES

The resources the environmentalists mobilized for the cause of sea turtles included organization, technical knowledge, finances, public sentiment, and access to and influence with policymakers. The ecology movement of the 1960s emerged in the seventies as a movement that had succeeded in energizing large segments of the public and staunch allies among policymakers.

The lesson learned in the 1960s was that the challengers who could mobilize resources could have an enduring impact. The successful group uses resources to garner more resources. Existing organizations were used to build more organizational strength. Favorable public sentiment was used to deepen the saliency of the cause. The knowledge base was expanded, and ideas proven successful were further perfected. Funds and workers were used to tap new sources and new members. Influence with policymakers was expanded.

By the 1970s the Center for Marine Conservation could tap an impressive array of resources. Besides the obvious financial resources, it drew upon public sentiment favorably disposed to protecting the environment. As a tangible and easy to comprehend issue, sea turtles could move public sentiment better than exhortations to clean up the water and air. And not only can people identify with this emotional issue, but it is easier still to garner support when the enemy of the endearing species can be villainized. Such was the case with maverick shrimpers who could not state their position in the polished prose of environmental lawyers. Indeed lower profile species will draw less interest, allowing hundreds of species of animals and plants to go unprotected. But choices are made according to the formula of proven success. The high profile species are more likely to evoke emotions, public sentiment, and financial support. It would, of course, be counterproductive were environmentalists unable to decide which species to protect. For this reason, organization is crucial for a successful challenge.

The decision to protect turtles was not the product of a democratic process. Members were not polled to determine whether they wanted sea turtles or sea worms protected. The decision was a product of a bureaucratic and oligarchical organization which depended on a network of organizations for moral and financial support. To be sure, every organization holds its own survival as its chief objective. This is the nature of organizations and is not unique to environmental organizations. All partners to an alliance will participate only if it is deemed in their interests. It takes skilled leadership to create consensus and cooperation. Organization is possibly the most valuable resource, but knowledge is also a boon.

The Center for Marine Conservation had the services of lawyers who were well connected with government—a key ingredient in the Center's success. Future successes became more likely as the ties between government and the corporation-friendly environmental groups grew. At the close of the acute phase of the TEDS conflict, Michael Weber accepted a position with NMFS at the national office in Washington, D.C.

Thus, the Center for Marine Conservation, like other environmental groups, have access to elites in government and in corporate America. And policymakers consult national environmental groups. In one sense, the Center for Marine Conservation and similar organizations seem to represent the environmental position of policymakers. To the extent that national environmental organizations foster closer ties with environmentally insensitive corporations, choose problems that are unthreatening to corporate America, and have the power to speak for the country on environmental issues, they are the policymakers. To that extent, one can say that the movement has been co-opted.

Chapter

7

Leisure and Coastal Development

In the last two decades, a significant transformation of America has taken place. Not only have urban populations moved to the coast, but land use patterns have shifted from traditional farming and fishing to a variety of recreational uses. These trends have not been uniform over time, nor have they occurred at the same rate over coastal America. But almost everywhere, some evidence of this transformation can be discerned. Commercial fishing and farming communities are giving way to new land and water use patterns.

As Americans acquire more leisure time and resources, the recreational industry has expanded. Coastal America offers a respite from crowded urban centers with its beaches, water sports, and other amenities. But traditional farming and fishing communities represent a land use pattern somewhat at odds with condos, marinas, leisure resorts, and retirement communities. How land and water is used, of course, is not only subject to market forces; social policy also plays a significant role. Local and state governments may encourage or discourage particular land use patterns. The question is how and why are these decisions made? This chapter focuses on the consequences of land and water policy. However, it is relevant to the issue that social policy is not merely an expression of the public will, but the ability of successful groups to get what they want—in this case, to determine how marine resources will be used. It is also germane that local and state governments assist, resist, or merely stand by and watch. The transformation of coastal America, therefore, involves power, and the power to determine how the marine environment will be used is not in the hands of harvesters who presently depend on the bounty of land and sea. Past changes on the coast and those poised to make their debut comprise the milieus in which the TEDs drama has been played.

In examining these milieus, commercial marine harvesters appear to have become vulnerable to the forces of change. Since change in America is usually called progress, the traditional practices of commercial harvesters are in conflict with other more modern uses of marine resources. The most intense and virulent conflict occurs between commercial harvesting and sportfishing. The purpose of this chapter is to examine the conflict between these two competing users of marine resources.

It is possible that the conflicts between commercial harvesters and recreational interests and the present social and economic trends are creating challenges to commercial harvesters which could end in the economic demise of commercial fishers.

ORGANIZED SPORTFISHING INTERESTS

As long as recreational fishers were unorganized, commercial harvesters faced little competition from them. Scattered fishing and boating clubs had neither the resources nor the organizational focus to challenge commercial harvesters. But arrangements changed with the emergence of the Gulf Coast Conservation Association.

The GCCA had its beginnings in 1977 in Texas when fourteen sportfishing entrepreneurs met in a Houston sporting goods store to launch a sportfishing organization. Among them were Walter Fondren, Jr., and Perry Bass. Fondren's father had founded Humble Oil Company. Fondren served as chairman of the Gulf of Mexico fisheries and Management Council. Perry Bass, a member of the Fort Worth, Texas, Bass family whose fortune is based in oil and banking, served as director of Texas Department of Natural Resources. Both Fondren and Bass are serious yachters, and Fondren has been involved with yacht-building and sales. TSA board member Deyaun Boudreaux claimed:

> [Fondren founded] two environmental organizations . . . GCCA and Ducks Unlimited. He formed Ducks Unlimited when he was the executor for a large land holding in south Texas that was located between two waste sites owned by ChemWaste. . . . Fondren invests in resorts and boating interests. One of his sidelines is gambling in the form of organizing calcuttas. . . . a group of people buy a yacht and hire a professional crew to work the international fishing tournaments. . . . they raise a large pot of up to $750,000 for the boat that catches the largest fish [marlin].[1]

Some in the shrimping industry question Fondren's motives and argue that his conservationism is suspect, since he allegedly owns the land in Calhoun County,

A Gulf Coast Conservation Association billboard depicts a speckled trout and a red drum, previously bread-and-butter species of commercial fishers and the most favored among local restaurateurs. In addition to a moratorium on red drum, which is still in effect, gamefish status for these two species would be a serious blow to commercial fishers.

Texas, which was to serve as a depository for fly ash from ocean incineration.[2]

Within eight years of its founding in Texas, GCCA had established itself in nine southern coastal states, from Virginia to Texas, with each regional group having considerable autonomy. Following expansion, an umbrella organization, the Coastal Conservation Association (CCA), was created as a watchdog of fishing activities and a lobbying force for recreational fishing interests. Through political influence, the CCA attempts to work with state wildlife and fisheries agencies as well as federal marine regulatory agencies in developing programs and legislation that protect and enhance the fishing resources for recreational fishers. According to a GCCA brochure, in 1988 the CCA had 40,000 members and boasted that 64 percent of its membership had a family income of over $50,000.

COMPETITION BETWEEN RECREATIONAL AND COMMERCIAL SECTORS

The conflict between recreational and commercial sectors is focused on marine species targeted by recreational and commercial harvesters and on land use, chiefly, fishing and farming as opposed to other land uses.

In the Gulf red drum, speckled trout, red snapper, and other species are objects of competition. These are highly favored species by both recreational and commercial harvesters. The Gulf of Mexico Fishery Management Council placed a moratorium on commercial harvesting of red drum. Since 1990 the Gulf of Mexico

Fisheries and Management Council has pushed bycatch reduction. That is, this effort regulates the shrimp fishery to reduce juvenile finfish incidentally taken in shrimp trawls and limits the number of red snapper taken by red snapper fishermen. Provisions affecting shrimpers were postponed until 1994. Since then, the Council has been considering a variety of options, including bycatch reduction devices (BRDS). From the commercial harvesters perspective, more and more species are being set aside for recreational fishers, leaving fewer species for commercial harvesters. From the recreationists' point of view, this represents a sensible approach to conservation. The impact of this trend on shrimpers, although hard to quantify, is substantial. A majority of shrimpers in our sample landed other species (table 2). Other species (fish and crabs) are used to supplement income and maintain family sustenance. The economic return from bycatch in the Gulf has not been measured. One study of South Atlantic shrimpers concluded that bycatch is important for shrimpers.[3] Existing data, however, are inadequate to measure the Gulfwide and South Atlantic impact of the loss of bycatch to shrimpers. Generally, the smaller the boat, the more important the bycatch, because all the catch (mostly crabs and edible fish) can be sold or utilized by kin and neighbors.

COMPETITION OVER LAND USE

Competition over land use varies by state depending, at least in part, on the topography. Generally, coastal development is an expansion of recreational, leisure, and tourist use patterns. In the wake of intensive coastal development, commercial harvesting is likely to be replaced. If for no other reason, economic factors favor usages which, when taken in their entirety, return more. A small strip of coast with condos, marinas, and other amenities is likely to bring a greater economic return. Policy makers cannot ignore that benefit. Arguably, as some studies claim, recreational fishing returns more than commercial fishing.[4] But in some states the leisure and tourist industry has a larger economic value than the commercial fishing industry and receives more attention from policymakers. It is, therefore, not surprising that fishing and farming have given way to recreational usage and real estate development.

LOUISIANA AND FLORIDA: DIFFERENT EXPERIENCES

Louisiana and Florida have different levels of coastal development.

THE LOUISIANA CASE

Although shrimpers from North Carolina to Texas are aware of the threat they face from sportfishing, Louisiana provides an excellent example of development in its earliest stages.

The decline in oil and gas industry in the Gulf has prompted an economic motive for the State to attract other industries. A leisure and tourist industry, already well established in Florida, is making its appearance in coastal Louisiana. But Louisiana's topography is shaping its coastal development.

As one approaches the coast from the Gulf, slivers of abandoned beachfronts, called *cheniers*, protect the coastline. From here, more of the Gulf must be crossed before stretches of marsh of recent geological origin appear. Shallow bays and lakes abound. Numerous streams, including the Mississippi and Atchafalaya rivers, empty their burden of silt from the heartland of America. It is a remarkable system of estuaries and one that is ideal for spawning numerous marine species. But, though it is uniquely suited as fishing and shrimping grounds, it offers few of the amenities of coastal environments found along other areas of the American coast. There are no white sands or blue water, and the beaches are accessible only by boat. And although there are only a few condos or retirement communities, there is fishing twelve months of the year.

But Louisiana's topography is not its only claim to uniqueness; it has a singular social and cultural history as well. Its language, customs, and traditional practices set it off sharply from the rest of America. In some ways, the settlements of coastal Louisiana are both physical islands and social islands in an Anglo-Saxon sea. Its physical and social isolation has been a barrier to coastal development. Even after the development of offshore oil, Louisiana is at or near the bottom on most indicators of progress (average income, education, unemployment, poverty etc.).

THE FLORIDA CASE

The white sand and blue water beaches of Florida are markedly different from the marshes of Louisiana and Texas. Recreational use of the coastal zone in Florida has increased geometrically in the last several decades. A variety of social, economic, and demographic factors have led to this development. In its wake traditional fishing and farming communities have been disappearing and are being replaced by luxury motels, condominiums, and marinas. Indicative of Florida's recreational and tourist emphasis, the Florida Fishery Commission has recently initiated negotiated rulemaking to include a specific distance from the shore gear can be used.[5] The ban on using fishing nets near condos and marinas illustrates the conflict between the two use patterns. It also illustrates the relative power of the contestants in that the recreational industry has managed to set the agenda. Conceivably, Florida's planning committees could be meeting to set limits on beach development in order to preserve the livelihood of its commercial harvesters.[6] Consequently, the size of the shrimp fleet in Florida has dwindled, and the number of fishing villages has dramatically decreased. Similar trends are in the making in the Carolinas and in Georgia.

The level of coastal development may be related to the level of resistance to TEDS and other regulations, since there has been more resistance in Louisiana than in Florida.

Federal officials were tempted to assign some blame to Louisiana, and some have suggested that were it not for Tee John Mialjevich, shrimpers from other states would have accepted TEDS. Some also believed that Louisiana marine agents were not doing as good a job as were other agents. In the words of one government official, "shrimpers (in Florida) were ready to accept TEDS, but Tee John and his Louisiana gang came in and stirred them up."[7] A recreationist claimed that Louisiana shrimpers "let themselves be manipulated".[8] But perhaps the negative stereotype of Louisiana helped rationalize an explanation for a problematic management decision. Accordingly, some managers, scientists, and recreational interests have also characterized Louisiana's commercial harvesters as backward, volatile, and fickle, reflecting not only the stereotype but the social class difference between the two combatants. An alternative explanation for the intense resistance from shrimpers and state officials of Louisiana is that commercial harvesting is a major economic activity in the state. Surprisingly, many observers expressed shock over the effective way Louisiana harvesters used the political process to resist TEDS. But shrimpers were merely using the same political means during an impending crisis as other groups had routinely used. One need not subscribe to the unique Louisiana thesis to explain the level of resistance to TEDS and the sportfishing lobby among Louisiana shrimpers. We found the same attitude among shrimpers from the Carolinas to Texas. The difference is that TEDS impacted more people in Louisiana than elsewhere. Politically, the state of Louisiana could do nothing else but fight TEDS. With state backing, shrimpers were encouraged to carry on their resistance. This explanation of resistance seemed to escape the Department of Commerce.

Despite the bitter dispute over TEDS, commercial shrimpers and fishermen feel their real challenge is from elite recreational fishermen. "This is a class struggle," argued the president of the Southeast Fisheries Association.[9] The Terrebonne Fishermen's Organization president added: "The recreational fishermen [are] trying to put shrimpers out of business. The GCCA . . . wants to get all nets out of the Gulf."[10] Interestingly, the ad campaign waged by Gulf Coast Conservation Association (GCCA) in Louisiana included highway billboards with pictures of a red drum and a speckled trout. The solitary caption read, "The future is game fish." Had these two species been game fish, commercial harvesters could not have sold them.

But commercial harvesters are not alone in believing that the recreational elite are trying to eliminate their industry. Privately, government officials have drawn the same conclusion. Although all categories of state and federal officials involved with fisheries mention the anticommercial attitude of the sportfishing lobby, Sea Grant Extension agents were most ready to volunteer comments: "Shrimpers have more of a threat from the sportfishing lobby than from environmentalists. These groups admitted to me that they don't want any nets in the Gulf. They have money and the leisure time to work on their goals."[11] Another agent volunteered his analysis of fishery management: "You have to remember that you can't confuse the environmental movement with the conservation/sportfishing movement. These people are after something. Originally, the councils were created by concerned citizens/ sportsfishermen types. They were big on sportfishing. They took an anticommercial fishing stance. Eventually they adopted the politics of fishery management."[12] Another marine agent added, "Coastal development is turning the corner everywhere from commercial to recreational emphasis."[13]

FROM SPORTFISHING TO COASTAL DEVELOPMENT

In order to explain how sportfishing and coastal development are related, one has to examine the growth process. Substantial amount of research has documented the way the growth machine operates.[14]

According to Logan and Molotch, land speculators work closely with local governments and local elites to change land use patterns for profitability. Local elites and local governments are committed to growth because they too stand to gain. The job of local governments and local elites is to promote growth as a benefit to the entire community. Thus, they must mold public opinion, silence the opposition, and create organizational bridges between the holders of capital and the power of government.[15]

The individuals and groups whose lives are organized around the present use of the land will oppose growth (fishers and farmers are examples). But because they have less resources, cannot influence government the way elites can, and often lack the sophistication to mount a challenge, they cannot prevent growth. The promise that growth will benefit everyone and is good for the community is not sustainable. The effects of growth is that some profit while others have their lives disrupted.[16] Although Logan and Molotch have focused on land development in cities, their analysis applies to coastal development as well. The formation of alliances between elites and the government is the same whether one examines land development in cities or coastal development. One difference worth noting is that in coastal development, the elites are using conservation as the justification to introduce coastal development.

DOMESTIC COLONIALISM

We are inclined to see the growth machine as a form of domestic colonialism because elites bring in capital, alter land use patterns, and use the resources of the area for their own gain. If this benefits locals, so much the better. If it does not, elites cannot be held responsible for impersonal market forces.

INVISIBLE HANDS OF PROGRESS

Progress always seems to be uneven, rapid in one place and creeping along in another.[17] If a country or region is backward, some assume the people who live there are so.

In colonialism economic exchanges can be very unequal. Under colonialism the rich countries take more than they gave. In many ways they not only profit from the misery of poorer countries, their actions actually create the misery, which is precisely what Pope John XXIII exhorted developed nations to avoid. In his papal encyclical, *Mater et Magistra,* Pope John XXIII cautioned developed countries to "take care lest, while giving help to less developed nations, they turn the political situation that prevails there to their own profit or imperialistic aggrandizement. If such an attempt be made, it must be explicitly labeled as an effort to introduce a new form of colonialism, which, however cleverly disguised, would be only a repetition of that old, outdated type from which many peoples have recently escaped."[18]

Relations among countries can be skewed so that the powerful dominate the weak. By the same logic, there can exist dominant-subordinate relations within nations.[19] One region prospers, in part, because of misery in another region. Under these conditions, a domestic or internal colonialism prevails. The poorer region comes to depend on the largesse of the prosperous region. Historically, the South has been in a subordinate relationship with the financial centers in America.

No more poignant description of dependency in the South can be found than in Harry Caudill's *Night Comes to the Cumberlands.* Stressing the role of absentee owners, Caudill describes how coal mining has extracted more than coal from the Appalachians. The region stands out as an extraordinary example of the effects of dependency. But it is not an isolated case in the South. Some argue that recent industrialization in the new South has brought fewer benefits than attendant costs. Industrial development has not reduced the economic gap between the South and the North. Wages are still lower and the South has had to compromise some of its environmental integrity.[20] Industrial practices not tolerated in other parts of the country are acceptable in parts of the South. Similarly, working conditions and wages have been compromised.

Since the Civil War the economy in the North has dominated the South, and this domination has been centered in the largest northern cities. Thus, if one can say that the South is not in the core economy, the rural South is even more peripheral. Yet, industrial development in the South has been characteristically outside large urban areas, and its negative impact can be seen in the rural areas.[21] But the cues taken for these changes originate in large cities.[22] According to Hawley, "A relatively simple way of characterizing the relationship between the metropolis and the settlement in the territory around it is as one of dominance and subordination. [Through its] processing, marketing, and administrative activities, the metropolis regulates the amount of wealth that enters the region, defines the kind of complementary units that are needed, sets the rhythm and the tempo of activity in the area, and influences the types of people who congregate there."[23]

An excellent example of urban dominance can be seen in laws restricting the killing of certain species. Once acceptable and, indeed, necessary for the survival of rural folk, the killing of wild game begins to have a new social meaning. As a large urban middle class moved into a previously rural area, the nature of wild game changed from an activity that supplies food for the family table to a type of weekend recreation. To the rural folk, hunting is interwoven in the fabric of life; it serves many functions. To the affluent urbanite, hunting is either a cruelty or merely a sport. Conflict emerges as the more affluent urban migrants begin to exert their values over rural society. Rural residents come to find long-standing traditional practices have become illegal, as wild game, once the common resource of rural folk becomes the weekend sport of an urban middle class.[24]

But urban dominance affects more than game laws; it widens the gap between the developed urban areas and the less developed regions. It does so by taking advantage of regional "backwardness" and alters the rural environment by infusing money for development. The new capital does not have the same effect as in the urban core.

How is capital used in the core and the periphery? What are the workplace differences in the two sectors? How are these economic factors translated into power factors? To oversimplify the answers, there are two economies.[25]

Capital from the core invested in the periphery is selective so as to profit from the abundance of a natural resource or a cheap labor supply. Stable high-paying jobs of the core are not created. Firms conducting business in the periphery take advantage of tax breaks, relaxed environmental standards, a more poorly educated, and thus cheaper, labor supply, and antiunion local and state governments. Furthermore, the "backward" areas are often the site of extractive industries. The minerals and the capital flow from the periphery to the core. Coal mining in Appalachia or oil and gas production in Louisiana are good examples.

Along American coasts still dominated by farmers and fishers, capital is less available than in cities, the work environment is of a lower quality (lower pay, poorer working conditions, less job security), the farmers and fishers are racially and/or culturally identifiable, and the backwardness of the area can be conveniently explained away.

The EPA had designated areas off the coast of Texas for ocean incineration. The wastes would have gone through Lake Charles, Louisiana. People who fish and shrimp for a living and local environmentalists fought the plan, and for the time being, wastes were not burned in the Gulf.[26] Although it is unthinkable to suggest burning wastes off the coasts Florida or California, if it serves the national purpose to get rid of wastes, the waste is placed in a location where the least opposition exists.

For the same reason, the fishery policy decisions made in Ottawa served the interests of the more developed regions of Canada at the expense of economically depressed Newfoundland.[27] Similarly, the local and state coastal policy in Florida has enhanced the leisure and tourist use of the Florida coast at the expense of traditional commercial harvesters.[28]

THE WINDS OF CHANGE ARE BLOWING

Visitors and settlers from the urban centers have usually followed the development of oil in Texas and Louisiana and lumber along the South Atlantic. They come to view the scenery, fish, or escape the deteriorating environment of cities. In parts of coastal America, and Canada, too, newcomers and native elites are changing the coast. Through the process of rural gentrification, urban migrants have come to exercise increasing influence over decisions affecting use of coastal rural resources.[29] These newcomers have the means and the know-how to pressure local government for change.

There are parallels between the dominance exerted by a relatively small elite over marine resource allocations in the Gulf and other policy decisions made in coastal America. Many middle-class and upper-class migrants to rural coastal America have recently made an impact on land use patterns. Their presence and influence in largely traditional fishing and farming communities has been steadily increasing. They are in conflict with fishers, in some cases, over land use much the way sportfishing organizations are in conflict with commercial fishers over marine species.

A growing body of information supports the notion that migrants to rural coastal America are altering land use patterns. They bring an urban ideology that favors a recreational and aesthetic use of resources.[30] These values are not altogether inconsistent with their economic interests, particularly the maintenance of property values. What researchers have discovered is that the affluent migrants and natives to coastal America prefer recreational uses of land, and since the affluent are more likely to move to the coast, the trend favors recreational use.[31] Their influence over the decision-making process is often exerted to the detriment of working-class natives—privatization of land and recreational use of marine resources.[32]

The exurbanites have found allies among affluent natives. In coastal Virginia tensions between migrants and natives is confounded by the "emergent unequal distribution of scarce waterfront property and its subsequent privatization."[33] Similarly, in coastal Maine migrants and affluent natives share common attitudes toward growth management and these attitudes stem from their affluent background.[34]

What has emerged is a coalition between migrants and affluent natives, natives whose interests and values are more attuned to national and international interests and who have a more cosmopolitan outlook. The gentrification of rural coastal America is creating new opportunities for native cosmopolitans to alter the allocation of resources. The land use changes are more consistent with their economic interests and the interests of the exurbanites.

Paradoxically, the influx of migrants, which has been both the cause and effect of development, into rural coastal America unleashes conservative nongrowth forces. It is the rural amenities that attracts the newcomers in the first place, but the aesthetics and environmental qualities, as well as property values, are jeopardized by unrestrained growth. Thus, their interests are opposed to encouraging the kind of growth that would provide jobs for working-class locals. Growth management plans spearheaded by cosmopolitan locals and migrants are directed at preserving the aesthetic qualities of the coastal zone. Such management encourages privatization and recreational use of the coast. In Louisiana this process has only recently begun. The importance of commercial fisheries to the state's economy, the large number and diversity of commercial harvesters, and the unique topography of its coast have resisted this transformation. However, recent fishery regulations have restricted commercial harvesting of some marine species.

We have examined the TEDs conflict within the larger context of social change in coastal America. It is difficult to imagine how traditional fishers will survive in their present numbers in the future. The forces of change seem stronger than their power to resist. Ultimately the coasts will be transformed (unless a national policy blocks it), and there will be little room for commercial harvesters.

This process has been dramatically played out in coastal Mississippi.[35] In 1993 casino gambling interests quickly took advantage of the gridlock over awarding a casino contract in New Orleans and resistance to casino gambling from coastal Alabama residents. Mississippi has restricted gambling to water-based casinos, and a scramble for waterfront property immediately followed. Casino interests have pushed all incompatible land uses off the now more valuable beachfront property, and shrimpers were immediately under siege. Once the prime port for Mississippi shrimpers, Biloxi has become the gambling mecca of the Gulf coast. Ice houses and shrimp docks have been bought out and pushed into the back bays of Biloxi where a drawbridge separates the bay from the Gulf of Mexico. Due to the increase in tourism and attendant traffic, the drawbridge that links the interstate with the coast may be opened only for two one-hour periods in the morning and late evening. There were not enough shrimp houses for processing the good shrimp harvest of 1993. One Mississippi shrimper lamented, "You can't stop it [encroaching development] because it's money. . . . This is going to devastate our industry. Where are we going to go? Where are we going to go to unload, to get ice? This is my home. I'm sixty years old. If I was thirty, I could just hit the road like a gypsy, but I want to be with my family."[36]

As tourism and traffic increases, the drawbridge, the shrimpers' only link to the Gulf, may become more restrictive. A long-time stable industry of the Mississippi Gulf Coast is literally being moved out of sight.

But change is prevalent along the coasts of America, and fishers may not be able to resist its forces. Where they do survive, it will be because their way of life is saved as a living museum. Here and there on America's coast, small numbers of shrimpers will be encouraged to engage in their craft as a calculated ambience for a thriving leisure and tourist industry.[37]

Where extractive industries persist, leisure development of the coast will be slow and commercial harvesters will not be directly challenged. But that scenario suggests problems with water quality and marketability of catch. Globally, the large markets will be supplied with seafood produced by aquaculture. Technological development in aquaculture, conservation, and environmental policy, and the economic interests of elites will alter the way the marine environment is used.

With the decline of oil production in the Gulf, new sources of revenue are sought. We can expect to see tourism get a big push. The leisurely tours through the bayous and swamps of Louisiana have already begun. Coastal development aimed at a leisure class is also beginning to change the coast of Louisiana. Inevitably, tour boats and yachts will encounter head wells and exposed pipe, the legacy of a retreating oil industry. Commercial harvesting and the traditional way of life it supported face an uncertain future.

Chapter

8

Laws, Conflict, and Organizational Response

The conflicts that enveloped conservation and environmental laws of the last two decades reflect the unresolved national dilemma between environmental protection and economic enhancement. Two lines of conflict can be discerned not only in the TEDS case but in other resource conflicts as well. This chapter chronicles these two lines of conflict and the organizational responses harvesters made to the emergence, development, and expansion of the conflict surrounding the implementation and enforcement of the Endangered Species Act (1973) and the Fisheries Management and Conservation Act (1976).

UNRESOLVED NATIONAL DILEMMA

A successful environmental movement raised the consciousness of the nation by the late 1960s, and protecting the environment has become as much a part of the American ethos as our democratic ideals. This movement has won a thousand battles, but the eventual outcome of the war remains undecided. Its educational slogans are still left to be translated into workable national goals. In some ways, the movement is still incapable of reconciling environmental protection goals with the political and economic national purpose. How can a domestic policy of economic growth and expansion be realized in the context of environmental protection policy? Must jobs and the material quality of life be sacrificed to ensure a sound environment? Are Americans willing to pay the social and personal costs of environmental protection? How can these costs be distributed equitably? These are questions for which Americans have not yet developed consensus. There is, however, growing support for the belief that environmentally sound policy is not antithetical to economic progress. But, even if all Americans accepted the proposition that economic progress can best be achieved through sound environmental progress, would we have the will to make the short term sacrifices? Could we collectively agree to curb our consumerism and be content with some austerity? Even so, it would not cure all of our ills. Environments do not end at national boundaries.[1] Can we sell the same austerity to developing countries? Furthermore, how can we pursue the goal of political stability for Third World countries, stimulating their economies in an environmentally sound way?

Conflicts over environmental issues arise from the fragmentation of purpose with which Americans face environmental concerns.[2] Should the environment be preserved because it has intrinsic worth apart from its use value, as preservationists believe? Or should it be protected and conserved because of its use value to humans, as conservationists believe. Tension between these two purposes has been evident in government policy for at least one hundred years as resources were increasingly coming under the influence of government control and supervision.[3] Although national polls reflect a growing consensus of support for the environment on the part of Americans,[4] there is far less agreement on how that support translates into policy and how policy goals should be implemented. In short, everyone wants a good environment, but no one agrees on a single definition or means of financial support.

Conflicts over environmental issues spring from the tension between environmental protection and economic development.[5] The ambivalence with which Americans approach nature has given rise to laws that both mirror and contribute to the tension between these two nationally sanctioned mandates.[6]

The inconsistencies between environmental laws which espouse preservation values and conservation laws which espouse utilitarian or use values have made regulation and implementation problematic. Furthermore, tension between environmental protection and economic development exists within both types of laws as well as between each type.

Environmental protection laws enacted during the last three decades are themselves both a product of the conflict and attempts to resolve it. The Endangered Species Act of 1973 is largely a prohibitive law whose obvious intent is to protect endangered and threatened species and critical habitat.[7] It has repeatedly sputtered during its legislative history as a result of political pressure applied and targeted at its most vulnerable characteristic—the problematic approach it uses in addressing the social impacts of species and habitat protection.

ESA was intended to protect endangered species and habitats. It is clearly preservationist law but is not wholly without incongruous elements. These elements have been problematic for the implementation of the law. The allowance of exemptions and exceptions has invited the introduction of nonbiological factors in the decision making of implementation. The Alaskan natives whose subsistence depends on taking prohibited species were exempted as were certain hardship cases. The law provided Alaskan natives with a written exemption application.[8] Furthermore, ESA frontstaged the importance of critical habitat. In doing so, it increased the chances that conflicts would arise with projects that impacted land and water use patterns. The snail-darter and the critical habitat on which it depended blocked the expensive Tellico Project. Inevitably, lawsuits were filed, with claimants arguing that the high economic costs already expended and the benefits already forsaken were being wasted to preserve a tiny fish that had no use value. District courts did not resolve the conflict.[9]

Not surprisingly, in 1978 Congress amended the Endangered Species Act to include an oversight committee. The Endangered Species Interagency Committee, also called the God Squad, was empowered to determine whether projects under review should be exempt from federal prohibitions.[10] In the same session, Congress amended ESA to require economic impacts in any determination process to designate a critical habitat. The immediate impact was a drastic reduction in the number of listings and alarm among environmentalists that the effectiveness of the Act had been compromised. Meanwhile, the Tellico Project and the fate of the snail darter were argued all the way to the Supreme Court. The Court referred the question of costs and benefits to the newly created Endangered Species Interagency Committee. The Committee gave thumbs down to the Tellico Project, and for a while advocates for strict protection of endangered species were elated. The Tellico Project, however, was eventually attached to an omnibus bill and signed into law in 1979.[11] The conflict was eventually resolved at the highest levels of government.

No doubt the 1978 amendments were attempts to build in a mediation and review process. After a period of declining listings, Congress amended the Act in 1982. The new amendments removed those provisions that invited economic and social consideration in the determination decisions in the designation of critical habitat. These amendments notwithstanding, pressures still exist for governments to consider the economic and social costs of restrictions mandated by the Endangered Species Act. These pressures result in continuing conflicts severe enough to require resolution at higher levels. This was the case in the Tellico Project and it is the case with TEDS.

The Magnuson Act. The Federal Fisheries Conservation and Management Act[12] is intended to manage the marine resources for human use. Its principal dilemma is the difficulty of managing the resource for competing uses.

Although both acts seek to keep the environment viable, protection (ESA) and conservation (Magnuson) have quite different goals. The ambivalence in society between environmental preservation versus development is played out in the tension between the two acts. When five species of sea turtles were listed as threatened or endangered in the 1970s, environmentalists, using the provisions under ESA, sought their protection. Once it was established that significant numbers of sea turtles were incidentally taken in shrimp trawls, ESA provisions required some response from the regulating agencies. However, the National Marine Fisheries Service (NMFS) along with its parent agency, the National Ocean and Atmospheric Administration, regulated fisheries as required by the Magnuson Act. Their approach was to consider the social and economic costs of restricting the shrimp fishery.

The Magnuson Act was created to manage and conserve marine fishery resources out to two hundred miles. Its creation had two main functions: to remove the foreign fishing fleets from the United States' Exclusive Economic Zone (EEZ) and to establish a management system of regional councils. The councils were charged with establishing fishery plans and managing and conserving marine fishery resources in an equitable way for all user groups. Fishery plans must include social and economic impacts and are subject to the veto power of the Secretary of the Department of Commerce. By contrast, ESA is enforced by both the Department of Interior, chiefly the Fish and Wildlife Service (FWS) and the Department of Commerce. According to an established division of labor between the departments, the protection of sea turtles is the responsibility of the Department of Commerce.[13]

ESA policy does not require social and economic impact assessments as fishing plans under Magnuson do. However, a Magnuson protocol seems to have guided NOAA's and NMFS's attempt to protect endangered and threatened sea turtles. In the late 1970s and early 1980s, NMFS, with the aid of Sea Grant Extension Service, worked with the shrimp industry to find a solution which would have minimal negative impact on the fishery. Although the results of these efforts have been described in chapter three, this discussion underscores that the TEDS regulations are a hybrid of two quite different laws. From the very beginning then, TEDS regulations were immersed in the value conflicts within and between ESA and Magnuson.

Two lines of conflict can be discerned in the TEDS controversy, and these patterns are similar to other historical conflicts connected with the implementation of ESA and Magnuson. Besides being resolved at high government levels, the conflicts draw battle lines over the issue of social and economic impacts. Thus, they spawn myriad subdisputes around the original resource issue. Of course, the two tendencies are not mutually exclusive; they are treated separately here for economy of discussion.

WHAT GOES DOWN MUST GO UP:
ESA-TYPE DISPUTES

This upward path until resolution is achieved seems especially true of challenges to ESA and can be easily discerned in the TEDS case. Like the Tellico Project, the TEDS conflict was pushed upwards, but, unlike the Tellico Project proponents, shrimpers lost.

Similarly, the controversy over the spotted owl and old growth forests of the American Northwest is an ESA-type dispute. The lumber industry wants permission to cut virgin forests. Environmentalists have argued that cutting the virgin forest would lead to the extinction of the spotted owl. Until recently, environmentalists successfully blocked attempts by the lumber industry to harvest the old growth. After a protracted period of conflict, reminiscent of both Tellico and TEDS, the Endangered Species Interagency Committee ruled in favor of the lumber industry. In its successful attempt to win the right to cut old growth forests, the lumber industry was aided by other groups. One of the members of the coalition of injured parties of the Endangered Species Act was the Concerned Shrimpers of America. In all three conflicts, Tellico, TEDS, and the spotted owl, the highest levels of government became involved.

PRESERVATION AT WHAT COST?

The conflicts over social and economic costs of preservation and conservation have been long and bitter, and the histories of both ESA and Magnuson reflect it.

The numerous conflicts occasioned by ESA led to amendments that, according to environmentalist arguments, gutted the ESA. In 1982 because of a dramatic decrease in the number of listings of endangered species, ESA was amended again to "prohibit consideration of economic impact in listing decisions and ensure that listings and delistings are based solely on biological data."[14] Although some of the conflicts ESA spawned were centered around the biological consequences of recovery plans, the majority were over the social and economic impacts; existing or proposed use was blocked. The history of Magnuson followed a somewhat different path.

MAGNUSON-TYPE DISPUTES

In 1976 Congress achieved one of its two purposes in enacting the law. It kept foreign harvesters out of U.S. waters, but its second purpose, managing fisheries, has been less than successfully accepted.[15] The latter has spawned numerous regional controversies, and a number of fish stocks have been severely overfished.

The intent was to manage fisheries to achieve optimal sustainable yield. As long as the harvesters were few and the marine resource bountiful, conflict was minimal. As fisheries grew and the limits of marine stocks were reached, the fun of distributing resources gave way to the anguish of regulating them. "The early years were easy," noted one NMFS official.[16] Another echoed the same sentiments: "It was fun; we looked forward to the challenge and the possibilities that the [Magnuson] law offered. We would be able to test the ideas [e.g., managing stocks] that we had learned in school."[17] However, the regulatory mode under Magnuson was stressful. Following the initial enthusiasm of managing fisheries, the NMFS officials eventually came to face their jobs with a certain amount of dread, as no one wanted to confront the shrimping industry.

The source of their difficulties arose because Magnuson takes into account the social and economic impacts on competing user groups and the resolution of allocation questions in a fair and equitable way. Accordingly, fishery management plans (FMPS) were put into place to not only resolve the major resource issue (optimal yield) but disputes between user groups as well (e.g., shrimpers and recreational harvesters). Magnuson further requires the government to take into account the social and economic impacts a proposed regulation will have on a fishery. Because both ESA and Magnuson laws were being applied, the TEDS regulations had to take into account an endangered species (required by ESA) and the social and economic impact on shrimpers (required by Magnuson). Therefore, the environmentalists were telling the government to stop the shrimpers from taking turtles while the shrimpers were telling the government to consider the TEDS' negative economic impact. Therefore, the TEDS regulations are a hybrid of two laws, and ESA law takes precedence over Magnuson regulations.

If shrimpers do get relief from TEDS regulations, it will come in some form of congressional action. In 1992 Congressman William Tausin introduced H.R. 1490 to revamp the ESA. In a conservative Congress, many shrimpers are hoping the ESA will be modified.

Certainly, Tee John is hoping the law (ESA) will be changed through the lobbying efforts of the Political Action League (PAL) he formed in 1993. Wilma Anderson, former CSA vice president, has also initiated an organization, Alliance for America, whose purpose is to support extractive industries, such as shrimpers, farmers, miners, and lumber workers. Anderson claims that the shrimpers will continue to work with others who have been negatively affected by the ESA.[18]

The outcome of these efforts and the future of the shrimpers are uncertain. How the nation will resolve the dilemma between environmental protection and economic enhancement is equally unclear. What is clear is that the widening circle of conflict occasioned by TEDS is not over because the tension between protecting the environment and jobs remains. The TEDS conflict has helped to create and dissolve organizations. It has empowered and also stripped power from leaders. The drama and game continue and are embedded in the larger drama that pits preservation against conservation, protection of the environment against economic progress.

Epilogue

The tension between preservation and conservation can only be understood and its resource implications fully assessed by tracing its historical roots. Some scholars trace the mastery-over-nature attitude of Americans to the Bible,[1] but the biblical view also encourages reverence for nature. Both attitudes of mastery and reverence were maintained and balanced until the Middle Ages brought about an economic transformation of Europe.

In largely rural America, with a seemingly endless frontier, the effects of the expansion of industry did not become apparent until the nineteenth century. In the wake of crowded and polluted cities, deforestation, and wanton slaughter of wildlife, concern for nature and the environment manifested itself. This concern was not prompted solely by the negative impacts of unrestrained industrial expansion but by other social changes as well.

These social changes cannot be neatly linked to particular historical events, and for this reason they have been called cultural drift.[2] The drift was in the direction of greater equality among humans. Democratization of society in the West was clearly apparent by the beginning of the nineteenth century. It was the growing equality of conditions that de Tocqueville argued was the most important cause of the transformation of the mores. The mores were becoming more gentle precisely because people can see themselves in their equals more readily than they can in either their superiors or subordinates. He said, "There is no misery so deep nor happiness so pure, that it can touch our minds and move our hearts, unless we are shown ourselves under a different guise."[3] Therefore, as the barriers separating people broke down, a greater sensitivity to suffering arose. This collective compassion was not limited to the sufferings of humans but was extended to animals as well. The nineteenth century not only spawned movements to end slavery and child labor but also cruelty to animals. By the twentieth century, the "more gentle mores" awakened in the nineteenth century had become "institutionalized compassion."[4] Increasingly, human and animal victims of suffering were covered by the mantle of sympathy. The elaboration and expansion of this compassion has by no means been uniform, but it has been a thrust of societal change. The increasing sensitivity to human and animal suffering is an important element in under-

Like sardines in a can, the shrimp fleet is tightly stacked for the annual Blessing of the Fleet celebration in Morgan City, Louisiana, circa 1960. Decorated for the occasion, the vessels of wooden construction would be replaced by steel-hulled vessels by the 1970s.

standing the revulsion felt by many people to the incidental killing of sea turtles in trawls. At the same time, it also gives rise to the sorrow evoked in many when they learn the hardships shrimpers face occasioned by TEDS.

Today a sea turtle drowning evokes in many the same feelings only a few people experienced when draught animals were beaten by their owners in the nineteenth century. Increasingly, more and more forms of cruelty to animals are considered intolerable. Understandably, animals closer to humans in form or behavior are encompassed more readily within the mantle of compassion. In this context marine mammals, such as dolphins, porpoises, whales, and seals, often behave in humanlike ways. Not surprisingly then, the Marine Mammal Protection Act of 1972 singled out these forms for special attention. In some ways, the sea turtles evoked a similar, although by no means equivalent, concern among the general public.

The general trend of widening the circle of compassion to include more and more forms and of increasing sensitivity to animal suffering provides an extra-utilitarian reason for preservation. These values coexist with widely accepted attitudes to use natural resources for the benefit of humans. Indeed, the Marine Mammal Protection Act is both a deep expression of sympathy and concern over the incidental taking of dolphins by tuna seines and a recognition of utilitarian use value of marine resources. Although it works towards the prohibition of willful and incidental taking of marine mammals, the Act has admitted exceptions (Alaskan natives and incidental commercial taking) and has extended these exceptions by five-year intervals. The last extension expired in 1993.[5] No national consensus exists as to how preservation and conservation values can be balanced.

Because large tuna nets indiscriminately capture and kill marine mammals, an acceptable marine resource harvesting (tuna fishing) is in conflict with the legitimate concern to preserve species and prevent suffering. Similarly, but not directly comparable, are the use of land-based resources with attendant destruction of wildlife (lumber versus owls, mining and ranching versus wildlife in the Mojave). In varying degrees all of these examples parallel the TEDS controversy. Some may wish to add to this list general agriculture since farmers use pesticides to increase crop yields. But pesticide use inevitably involves the incidental taking of wildlife in addition to the targeted pests.

Somewhere in the collective consciousness of the American people, and perhaps in all of Western society, there is abiding concern for animals and the tendency to humanize other species. America has the distinction of being the first country to acknowledge the rights of animals by enacting legislation to protect them from cruel treatment. As early as 1641, Massachusetts Bay Colony prohibited cruelty to animals.[6] Since that time, organizations abound which are dedicated to preserving animal rights as well as those educating, indoctrinating, and civilizing those who would trample on the liberties of animals. But organizations also have flourished that promote the gaming, breeding, raising, slaughtering, butchering, and consuming of the skin, flesh, organs, and fur of animals. Our society has also elevated the status of some animals to that of companion, pet, and even surrogate therapist. We have granted special protection under local, state, national, and international prescriptions and proscriptions to many species. Anthropomorphic sentiment, or the zoological connection, as some have termed it, has expanded rapidly since the end of World War II and remains a source of mixed feelings for those on both sides of the issue.[7] These sentiments have resulted in some rather dramatic confrontations between the two. The impact of the anthropomorphic movement has already been keenly felt in the United States and other countries. Furriers have been significantly reduced in western countries, particularly Britain, where about two-thirds of British furriers have been permanently closed. There are limits, however, to the impact the animal rights movement can have before backlash occurs. As shrimpers see it, the turtle species is considered more important than the species of working America.

TEDS are symptomatic of a larger national and global dilemma which has spawned numerous resource conflicts. How one chooses to solve conflicts will, of course, depend on how one views the debate over preservation and economic enhancement. While we ponder these issues philosophically, the forces of change are already limiting our options. Some may view the recent, even future, changes as a matter of destiny and sit back stoically to watch the sea and landscape change. But we believe it is within the grasp of mortals, however imperfect and uncertain our methods, to mold the future. Whether we view change as the blind forces of fate or the product of collective decisions is crucial to the future of our natural resources. Regardless of how we come to phrase the problem, some will benefit immensely from the changes and others will bear the cost. Inevitably our decisions have moral dimensions. We believe that conflicts like the TEDS conflict will only be laid to rest when we resolve the larger issues. Until then, both turtles and shrimpers are in peril.

Appendices

APPENDIX A
THE SAMPLING PROCEDURE

The primary sample of shrimpers involved a multistage strategy. The 1988 list of Louisiana licensees (those listing gear with which shrimp are taken) was used to identify the population. The first stage included a 1-in-50 systematic sample of the entire 18,000 licensees. The second stage involved stratifying the resultant 365 cases into three strata based on vessel size and the number of trawls. Vessels of 25 feet or longer pulling two or more trawls represent .096 of the primary sample. Vessels 25 feet or more with a single trawl represent .178 of the primary sample. The third stratum contained vessels under 25 feet and constituted .726 of the primary sample.

In order to have a sufficient number of each type of respondent to examine and compare, equal numbers of respondents (10) were drawn from each of the 3 very disproportionately sized strata. Accordingly, the large vessels pulling 2 or more trawls were selected with higher probability than the more numerous other two strata. From largest to smallest, the probabilities of selection are: $(.02 * .286)$, $(.02 * .154)$, $(.02 * .038)$. Finally, equal numbers of backup respondents, that is, those having the same characteristics (vessel size, number of trawls, geographical location), were selected from the 3 strata to be used as replacements for the initial sample if these individuals were unreachable. Because we desired equal numbers in each stratum, larger vessels were oversampled and small vessels were undersampled. However, the weighting procedure makes an adjustment for this distortion.

We intended to augment the primary sample with a snowball sample of protesters (seek the next respondent by asking the current respondent if they could recommend another person); however, this approach proved unsuccessful. At the time we attempted to locate protesters, many shrimpers feared reprisals and were reluctant to admit involvement. However, we were successful in getting informants to reconstruct the TEDs protest. We ultimately settled for a primary sample of 51 Louisiana shrimpers. The probabilities of selection from largest to smallest vessel are $(.02 * .371)$, $(.02 * .246)$, and $(.02 * .083)$. This sample was augmented with a quota sample of 16 non-Louisiana shrimpers. These shrimpers were interviewed on the docks and were used for comparative purposes only. Since this segment of the sample was not drawn randomly, population parameters of non-Louisiana shrimpers cannot be estimated. In addition to the above 67 shrimpers, other shrimpers were interviewed in a more limited way. These included leaders of commercial shrimping organizations both in Louisiana and in other Gulf and South Atlantic states as well as shrimpers who had participated in the TEDS agreement. However, this subsample was not used to estimate population parameters since selection was not random.

Finally, when findings are presented for the 51 respondents drawn from the 1988 license list, weights appropriate to their initial proportion in the population returns the sample to one representative of the population of Louisiana shrimpers. However, where comparisons are made between Louisiana and non-Louisiana shrimpers, it should be noted that since a nonrandom sample of non-Louisiana shrimpers was drawn, no population estimates are made or implied.

Estimates of the population (Louisiana shrimpers only) are reported in tabular form without confidence levels or intervals. In every case the confidence level is .05 (1 in 20). The confidence intervals range from .08 to .14, with the majority being near the .08 end.[1]

The following information includes findings of the survey and some documentary evidence (fleet sizes by state) relevant to the shrimp fishery. Our focus is the Louisiana shrimp fishery, however, non-Louisiana shrimpers are included and compared.

FINDINGS: SHRIMPER SURVEY

Size of the fleet. Estimating the size of shrimp fleets has been problematic. The National Marine Fisheries Service, the Coast Guard, and state agencies each report information on boats and vessels differently. Therefore, data on gear, vessels, and fishermen cannot easily be extracted from published reports of the various agencies. Attempts to collate different data bases have been difficult.[2] In estimating the sizes of state fleets, we used data from NMFS, the Coast Guard, and state agencies. We have tried to reconcile the differences and have rounded to the nearest hundred to reflect the lack of precision. The estimates include all motor-powered vessel class sizes for the most recent available data (1988–90) (fig. 1).

For the most part, fleets have decreased from previous highs in the early and middle 1980s. The most important exception has been the Louisiana fleet which increased at the close of the 1980 decade. However, current estimates indicate that the number of licensed shrimp vessels in Louisiana decreased in the early 1990s. This decrease could be as high as 2,000 vessels.[3] Accordingly, our latest estimate of

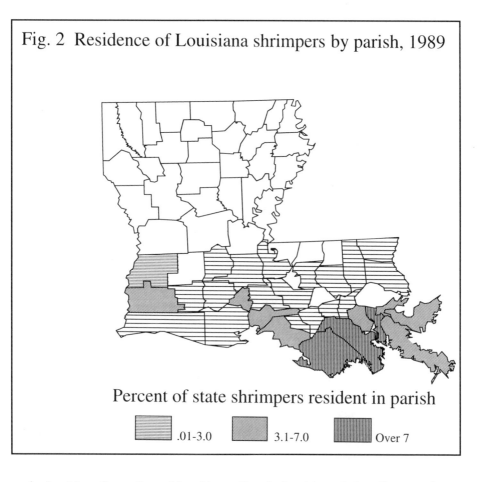

Fig. 2 Residence of Louisiana shrimpers by parish, 1989

Percent of state shrimpers resident in parish

.01-3.0   3.1-7.0   Over 7

the Louisiana fleet reflects this evidence. Yet, the Louisiana shrimp fleet remains not only the largest fleet but in some ways also the most diverse.

Louisiana shrimp fishery. Although all coastal and near-coastal parishes have resident shrimpers, they are concentrated in central coastal parishes. The parishes of Jefferson, Terrebonne, and Lafourche are conspicuously home parishes for nearly half of Louisiana's shrimpers (fig. 2). The importance of the central coast for Louisiana's shrimp fishery has remained constant. Yet, the shrimp fleet has experienced significant changes in recent years. Shrimping effort has increased, the value of shrimp has decreased, and newcomers have entered the fishery.[4] Presently, 3 percent of the fleet is Vietnamese, but nearly 10 percent of vessels over 60 feet are operated by Vietnamese. Furthermore, scores of native Louisianians entered the fishery from the late 1970s and the 1980s. Most of these newcomers operate small to medium-sized vessels. Part-time shrimpers outnumber full-time shrimpers and present a formidable obstacle to attempts to limit access. Shrimpers have made several attempts to initiate some form of limited access in recent years but have not been successful in finding a workable formula.

The majority of the nearly 18,000 Louisiana shrimpers shrimp in vessels under 25 feet in length (table 7). Vessel size in our sample varies from 16 to 87 feet. An examination of tables 1 and 2 reveals that the majority of Louisiana shrimpers have been residents in the State for 10 or more years, have a family history with shrimping, and have both friends and relatives who are involved in shrimping. Furthermore, the majority have been recruited into the fishery through kin (table 2), see shrimping as something more than a job (table 1), and identify autonomy (table 1) as the reason shrimping is attractive. Most have been in the fishery for 10 or more years (table 2). Only a fourth identify shrimping or other marine harvesting as their primary occupation, and a fourth reported oil and related work as their primary occupation. Few count themselves as members of commercial fishing organizations, and only a very small number describe themselves as highly involved with these organizations.

Fleet Diversity. Admittedly, the shrimpers of Louisiana are in some ways a diverse group. Some fish from small vessels, others employ large vessels (Vessel size reflects capital investment and, therefore, economic status; see table 7.). Part-time shrimpers outnumber full-timers by 3 to 1.

Market relations and problems. Only a fifth of the sample reported that they land only shrimp (table 2). But full-time shrimpers employing large vessels are more likely to land only shrimp and sell their catch to fish sheds. Nonetheless, shrimpers depend in varying degrees on other species, which may explain why shrimpers are prone to connect other fishery plans (e.g., red drum moratorium) with TEDs regulations. The implication is that the great majority of shrimpers have the ability to redirect their efforts to other species. Therefore, regulations on shrimping are likely to have unintended consequences on nontargeted species. Of course, offshore shrimpers are less able to respond to a changing regulatory climate. Because of the level of their capital investment and their larger-sized vessels, they find it more difficult to change gear and enter shallower waters. However, the extent to which the larger vessels land species other than shrimp has been underreported. In 1990 rumors abounded that the larger vessels were targeting finfish, particularly on their way back to home port.

Retail sales through customary outlets accounts and other forms of retailing, such as street hawking are more characteristic of the smaller vessels and part-timers (table 7). A significant percentage (38.0 percent) report that they do not sell their catch (table 3). Although a large component of the fishery can be loosely described as recreational shrimpers, there are reasons to believe that some of their catch winds up on the market. We will address this point in our discussion of limited entry.

There is variation in the disposition of bycatch. Only 16.7 percent of sampled shrimpers claim that their bycatch is thrown overboard (table 3). Some shrimpers report that their bycatch is sold (22.5 percent), and some report that it is kept for personal use (60.7 percent). That the majority of Louisiana shrimpers report some use value for their bycatch is consistent with findings from other regions. Kitner has reported that the majority of South Atlantic shrimpers utilize part of their bycatch and has estimated the annual value to be around $200.[5] These facts are relevant to bycatch reduction initiatives.

Few shrimpers report difficulty in selling their catch (table 3). However, most shrimpers feel that there are too many shrimpers. Significantly, the majority of the shrimpers accept, in principle, some form of limited entry as a solution to some of their difficulties.

ATTITUDES ON THE PROTEST

Since shrimpers see TEDS as a threat to their way of life, the majority agreed with the TEDS protest (table 4). However, the majority remained outside the circle of protesters. Less than half said that they knew a protester. The majority heard about the protest from the mass media. Only a fifth reported that they were encouraged to join the protest. These facts point to low involvement in the protest among sampled shrimpers. However, this is understandable given that the majority of protesters were offshore shrimpers, but the majority of Louisiana shrimpers fish the bays in small- to medium-sized vessels. Thus, it was vessel size and not lack of sympathy with the protest that precluded the majority of shrimpers from protest actions.

Although the majority of shrimpers (75.4 percent) believed the protest helped and an even larger number (86.0 percent) wanted TEDS repealed, most (77.5 percent) believed the regulation would remain the same (table 4). However, whether full- or part-time, educated or not, employing small or large vessels, and despite their relationship to the market, shrimpers unanimously saw TEDS as a threat (99.0 percent), a fact that is relevant to future management plans. It is a barometer of the extent that shrimpers can be mobilized in the future and an indicator of probable response to future restrictive regulations.

Shrimpers' assessments of groups that helped or hurt their cause during the conflict reveals a few anomalies. Understandably, Concerned Shrimpers of America was seen in positive terms. However, it is difficult to explain why the Louisiana Shrimp Association, buyers, and processors received high ratings (67.8 and 81.1, respectively). Because the economic interests of buyers and processors are different from shrimpers, one would expect shrimpers' attitudes to reflect this. Perhaps shrimpers had in mind only buyers from their own communities when they were responding to the question.

Other anomalies should also be noted in table 4. Although fishery scientists are typically employed by Sea Grant or NMFS, they were more favorably evaluated than either marine agents or NMFS officials. Few respondents were able to identify marine agents, but most had no trouble identifying NMFS. Not surprisingly, environmentalists were ranked lowest, but not that different from the ranking of NMFS officials. Clearly, the majority of shrimpers simply did not believe government people were helping shrimpers, but neither do they believe that organized labor helped. Only about 30 percent thought unions could have helped during the TEDS conflict.

The lack of faith in unions that shrimpers expressed is relevant to overtures by organized labor having been quickly turned down by the shrimper leadership. Perhaps leadership was echoing a sentiment held by the rank and file.

Attitudes about the protection of turtles and fishery regulations. Table 5 reveals that the majority of shrimpers do not feel turtles are endangered, and even fewer think shrimping endangers turtles. Yet, most feel that turtles can be saved. Interestingly, shrimpers feel that, if asked, they could develop ways to protect sea turtles. A majority describe themselves as having very unfavorable attitudes toward the enforcement of TEDS regulations.

The data illustrate that shrimpers do not perceive that they actually participate in the regulatory process. There is no evidence that they perceive public hearings as participation in rule making. That the industry has been called upon by government to suggest solutions to fishery problems is not perceived by the rank and file as their participation. These conclusions follow from the following considerations: (1) virtually every shrimper queried thought that shrimpers were not asked to suggest ways to protect turtles and (2) felt that they did not help decide regulations.

The majority felt that most shrimpers complied with regulations, and most reported they personally obeyed all regulations. The majority felt it was not stiffer penalties or consistent enforcement that evokes compliance. Respondents argued that both they and other shrimpers comply when regulations are fair. Although some regulations (TEDS) made no sense and were not fair, the majority still felt that in general past regulations were effective.

Finally, there is some sentiment in favor of compensation to shrimpers when regulations from which they receive no economic benefits are costly to shrimpers. For example, many shrimpers feel that they should be subsidized for pulling TEDS.

Conservation attitudes among shrimpers. During the TEDS conflict, shrimpers were forced to respond to comments that they lacked concern for the environment. Some of their responses were angry but did not reflect their true sentiments. Their attitudes are best exemplified by their actions, but for now we will examine shrimpers' responses to questions on conservation contained in the survey.

Table 6 reflects that a large percentage of shrimpers define nature as fragile, and about the same proportion see nature as resilient. Generally speaking, when one believes nature is fragile, one is inclined to protect nature. In contrast, when one believes nature is resilient, one is inclined to expect nature to heal itself. Most shrimpers believe in the efficacy of science. This fact suggests optimism; problems created by man can be solved by man.

Beyond sentiments and values, we asked about the attendant costs of conservation. Their responses indicate that they are both aware of and sensitive to costs associated with conservation. Nearly 84 percent were willing to accept general costs (high level plus moderate level of acceptance). When specific costs (loss of jobs) were mentioned, the acceptance level dropped (73.6 percent, high plus moderate levels). Finally, we asked shrimpers whether they were willing to accept personal costs. A majority (53.2 percent, high plus moderate levels) indicated they were willing to accept the personal costs of conservation. These data seem to suggest that (1) shrimpers recognize and accept the costs of conservation, and (2) they do not exclude themselves from among those who should bear those costs.

Finally, we tried to assess the shrimpers' overall conservation stance. We characterized their responses as one of three theoretical types. Table 6 ranks these conservation stances as high, moderate, and low. A respondent characterized as high expresses an awareness that conservation makes practical sense and that a disregard for the environment is imprudent. Forty-two percent are what we believed to be high conservationists. On the opposite side of the scale, we characterized 27.7 percent as having strident disregard (low conservation) for the environment. Of course, some shrimpers seem to combine aspects of both positions. The moderate conservation category, a residual category, includes 30.4 percent of the shrimpers.

Conservation attitudes of shrimpers are more meaningful in comparison with other respondents. On those attitudes that are comparable, Louisiana shrimpers are more conservation-minded than the general population but less so than environmentalists.[6] However, the extent to which environmentalists are willing to accept personal costs attendant to conservation is unknown. We know of no published research that has attempted to examine this issue.

Part-time and full-time shrimpers. A great deal has been said about the impact on the fishery by a large part-time contingent. The data presented in table 2 illustrate some of the differences and similarities between part-time and full-time harvesters. Comparable characteristics are also presented for non-Louisiana shrimpers. Caution should be exercised, however, when analyzing these data.

The sample of non-Louisiana shrimpers was not drawn randomly, but rather was a quota sample (selecting subjects that are available until the quota is reached). It would, therefore, be inappropriate to use these data to estimate the population of non-Louisiana shrimpers. In addition, percentages given for Louisiana shrimpers are based on small samples; therefore, more emphasis should be placed on the relative differences between part-time and full-time shrimpers than on the precise percentage differences between them. In other words, the data presented are more useful to gauge the differences between shrimper types than as a basis for estimating their exact percentages in the fishery. This caveat applies equally to the data presented in table 7. Yet, our estimate that 74.2 percent of Louisiana shrimpers are part-time is strengthened by the Baron-Mounce, Keithly, and Roberts estimate based on a sample of over 500 shrimpers.[7] They argue that the percentage of part-time shrimpers would have been significantly higher than the 60 percent they reported had shrimpers in all parishes of the state, rather than just the coastal parishes and those around Lake Ponchartrain, been interviewed.[8]

Our survey suggests that the influx into the fishery was more of a 1970s phenomenon than a 1980s one. If 80.0 percent of both part-time and full-time shrimpers have been in the fishery for 10 or more years, it is hard to draw any other conclusion, although it is possible for shrimping effort to have increased at a faster rate than the size of the fleet.

There is evidence that a segment of the part-time fleet is very different from the full-timers. More full-timers (90.0 percent) than part-timers (66.7 percent) have a family history of shrimping. Furthermore, a higher percentage of full-timers' relatives shrimp (90.0 percent) and closest friends shrimp (93.3 percent) than part-timers, whose corresponding percentages are 55.0 and 75.0, respectively. The fact that part-timers spend more time outdoors may be a function of the semirecreational nature of their relationship to the fishery. To be sure, part-timers are better educated and are more likely not to sell their catch. Furthermore, part-timers are more likely to keep part of their bycatch. Part-timers are also less likely to have been recruited into the fishery by kin and less likely to belong to commercial fishing associations but are more likely to belong to community associations. These data suggest that the part-time component of the fleet is a better educated middle-class person, not drawn from blue-collar ranks but rather with present or past white-collar job. Indeed, 55.0 percent fall in the "other" category of jobs held. These jobs include a wide variety of white-collar jobs and the professions. Interestingly, a substantial number of part-timers (35.0 percent) have held oil or oil-related jobs. This is comparable to the 40.0 percent of full-timers who have held oil and oil-related jobs.

Variation in vessel size. Understandably, the size of the vessel affects shrimping strategy. The smaller vessels usually remain within bays and shrimp for 24 hours or less. Baron-Mounce, Keithly, and Roberts report that the average trawling time is 10 hours.[9] Larger vessels will shrimp the coast and offshore in deeper water, remaining out for 7 to 10 days. Among our sampled shrimpers, most stay in the bays and along the coast (table 7). All of the shrimpers using small vessels, 73.3 percent using medium-sizes vessels, and 27.3 percent using large vessels identify themselves as bay shrimpers. Interestingly, even among shrimpers operating large vessels only 18.2 percent characterize themselves as deep-water shrimpers.

The evidence indicates that shrimpers employing small vessels are more likely to be new to the fishery. Although all categories of shrimpers are long-time residents of Louisiana, operators of small vessels are less likely to have a family history with shrimping (69.2 percent compared with 87.5 and 81.8 percent for shrimpers with medium and large vessels) and to have shrimped 10 or more years (53.8 percent compared to 75.0 and 77.3 percent for the other size categories). A slightly smaller percentage of small vessel operators' relatives (69.2 percent) and closest friends (69.2 percent) shrimp, but these differences are minimal; the corresponding percentages for operators of large vessels are 81.8 and 86.4. The small vessel operator is better educated but less likely to be a member of a commercial and community-based organization. However, he is similar in age and shares with his larger vessel counterparts an attachment to the profession (91.7 percent say shrimping is more than a job). Yet, despite these proshrimping sentiments, over 30 percent of the small-vessel operators, but less than 10 percent for the shrimpers in larger vessels, say they will not shrimp next year.

Occupational history by vessel size reveals that only 7.7 percent of small vessel operators consider shrimping their primary occupation. Corresponding percentages for shrimpers operating medium and large vessels are 56.3 and 90.9, respectively. Over 30 percent of the small-vessel operators hold oil and oil-related jobs. Much smaller percentages of shrimpers employing larger vessels hold oil and related jobs. However, job history of shrimpers for all vessel size classes is similar in one regard. About a third of all categories of shrimpers have held an oil and oil-related job. The smaller vessel operator is much more likely than shrimpers of other vessel size classes to have come to shrimping from a diverse occupational background (61.5 percent held occupations other than harvesting and oil). By contrast, a minority of shrimpers operating medium (46.7 percent) and large vessels (13.6 percent) held jobs outside of harvesting and oil and oil-related jobs.

APPENDIX B
TABLES

Table 1. Selected characteristics of Louisiana shrimpers

Characteristics	Unweighted Percent	Weighted Percent
Resident in La. for 10 or more yrs.	96.1	94.0
Family history of shrimping	80.4	73.8
Shrimping 10 yrs. or less	17.6	11.2
Primary occupation		
shrimping and related	58.8	24.8
oil and related	13.7	24.9
other	27.5	50.4
Other occupations held		
shrimping only	22.0	07.0
oil and related	38.0	37.4
other	40.0	54.4
Self-reported type of shrimper		
bay	60.0	88.0
bay and coast	32.0	10.1
deep water	08.0	01.9
Relatives shrimp	76.0	71.2
Closest friends shrimp	86.0	76.2
Shrimping provides autonomy	75.0	75.4
Shrimping is similar to harvesting	61.9	65.2
Shrimping is more than a job	87.0	89.9
Plans to shrimp next year		
full-time	50.0	20.7
part-time	36.0	54.8
will not shrimp next year	14.0	24.5
Would like children to shrimp	42.9	46.1
Under 50 yrs. old	57.1	49.3
Education		
some college	22.0	35.0
high school	32.0	36.8
grade school	46.0	28.2
Military or trade school	37.5	56.3
Membership in commer. fishing assoc.	44.0	18.7
high level of involvement	10.0	03.0
Membership in community associations	48.0	42.8

N=51

Table 2. Comparisons between non-Louisiana and Louisiana
full- and part-time shrimpers characteristics

Selected Characteristics	Non-Louisiana Total sample	Louisiana Full-time	Part-time
Resident in comm. 10 yrs. or more	100.0	96.7	95.2
Family history of shrimping	87.5	90.0	66.7
Shrimping 10 yrs. or more	93.8	80.0	80.0
Other jobs held			
shrimping only	62.5	36.7	N.A.
oil and related	0.0	40.0	35.0
skilled trade	18.8	16.7	10.0
other	18.8	06.7	55.0
Relatives shrimp	81.3	90.0	55.0
Closest friends shrimp	100.0	93.3	75.0
Spare time spent outdoors	81.3	62.1	90.0
Membership in community assoc.	56.3	37.9	61.9
Membership in commercial assoc.	75.0	60.0	20.0
Recruited by kin to fishery	81.3	83.3	52.6
Like to see children shrimp	56.3	48.3	35.0
Shrimp in bays only	0.0	37.9	90.5
Land only shrimp	25.0	40.0	17.6
Sell their catch			
fish shed	100.0	73.9	15.8
retail	0.0	08.7	21.1
other	0.0	15.2	26.3
do not sell	0.0	02.2	36.8
Bycatch is trash fish only	31.3	48.3	21.1
Disposition of bycatch			
throw overboard	25.0	41.4	16.7
sell some	75.0	41.4	16.7
keep some	0.0	17.2	66.7
Educational level			
some college	21.4	06.9	42.9
high school	42.9	34.5	28.6
grade school	35.7	58.6	28.6
	N=16	N=30	N=21

Table 3. Market relationships and problems facing shrimpers

Characteristic	Unweighted Percent	Weighted Percent
Land only shrimp	31.9	20.9
Sell shrimp to		
fish shed	42.9	14.6
retail	16.3	23.1
other	24.5	24.4
do not sell	16.3	38.0
Reported it is hard to sell catch	12.2	16.0
Had to give shrimp away	08.2	08.5
Bycatch is trash fish only	37.5	20.3
Dispose of bycatch		
throw overboard	31.9	16.7
sell some	31.9	22.5
keep some	36.2	60.7
Problems facing shrimpers mentioned		
TEDS regulations	98.0	94.5
too many shrimpers	64.7	66.8
low prices due to imports	58.8	33.0
closures	21.6	11.5
butterfly nets and skimmers	27.5	29.4
large vessels shrimping in bays	17.6	20.7
night trawling	25.5	19.4
poor catch and size	27.5	34.5
operating costs increasing	43.1	45.2
some groups trying to drive shrimpers out	07.8	02.5
non-TEDS regulations	23.5	22.1
coastal erosion and pollution	27.5	17.3
Recommends some form of limited entry	56.9	52.9

N=51

Table 4. Attitudes towards TEDs and the protest

	Unweighted Percent	Weighted Percent
TEDs are a threat to shrimpers	95.9	99.0
Agrees with the TEDs protest	72.9	86.0
Knows a protester	38.8	41.5
Heard about the protest		
from friends	53.2	38.8
from mass media	46.8	61.2
Knows how protest was organized	10.4	03.1
Encouraged to join protest	30.2	19.9
Stand on protest same as friends/kin	92.3	89.9
Thinks the protest helped shrimpers	63.6	75.4
Would like to see TEDs		
repealed	87.2	86.0
amended	08.5	02.6
stay the same	04.3	11.5
Believes the outcome of TEDs will be		
repealed	08.8	10.6
amended	14.7	12.0
stay the same	76.5	77.5
Believes shrimpers helped by:*		
CSA	91.4	78.5
La. Shrimp Association	82.4	67.8
buyers and processors	74.1	81.1
NMFS	10.7	14.8
Marine agents	52.6	34.0
Environmentalists	05.6	13.4
Scientists	50.0	59.5
Believes unions could have helped	28.3	29.7

* Half of respondents had no opinion, knowledge, or would not supply an answer.
N=51

Table 5. Attitudes about regulations and protecting turtles

Attitudes	Weighted Percent
Believes	
turtles are not endangered	56.6
shrimping endangers turtles	01.3
shrimpers were not asked to suggest ways	
to protect turtles	95.2
if asked, shrimpers could develop ways	84.1
sea turtles can be saved	71.7
shrimpers should be subsidized for pulling TEDS	68.7
shrimpers do no help to decide regulations	74.3
shrimpers have been asked to decide regulations	39.6
Believes shrimpers' compliance to regulations is	
high	61.3
moderate	26.7
low	12.0
Obeys all regulations	86.9
Compliance is influenced by	
regulations that make sense and are fair	63.7
stiffer penalties	08.0
consistent enforcement	28.3
Other shrimpers' compliance is influenced by	
regulations that make sense and are fair	55.1
stiffer penalties	16.0
consistent enforcement	28.9
Agrees regulations are efficacious	51.8
Assessment of TEDS enforcement is	
favorable	23.5
unfavorable	14.7
very unfavorable	61.8

N=51

Table 6. Attitudes about conservation

Attitude	Weighted Percent
Believes	
nature is fragile	44.1
resilient	44.6
somewhat fragile and somewhat resilient	11.4
science is efficacious	70.3
Acceptance of	
general costs of conservation is	
high	33.1
moderate	50.5
low	16.4
societal costs of conservation is	
high	40.0
moderate	33.6
low	26.4
personal costs of regulations	
high	18.2
moderate	35.0
low	46.8
General attitude to conservation is	
very favorable	42.0
somewhat favorable	30.4
unfavorable	27.7

N=51

Table 7. Selected characteristics of Louisiana shrimpers by vessel size

Characteristic	Small	Vessel Size Med.	Large
Resident in La. for 10 or more yrs.	92.3	100.0	95.5
Family history with shrimping	69.2	87.5	81.8
Shrimping 10 yrs. or less	53.8	75.0	77.3
Primary occupation			
shrimping and related	07.7	56.3	90.9
oil and related	30.8	12.5	04.5
other	61.6	31.3	04.5
Other occupations held			
shrimping only	0.0	20.0	36.4
oil and related	38.5	33.3	40.9
other	61.5	46.7	13.6
Self-reported type of shrimper			
bay	100.0	73.3	27.3
bay and coast	0.0	26.4	54.5
deep water	0.0	0.0	18.2
Relatives shrimp	69.2	73.3	81.8
Closest friends shrimp	69.2	100.0	86.4
Shrimping provides autonomy	75.0	78.6	72.7
Shrimping is similar to harvesting	70.0	41.7	70.0
Shrimping is more than a job	91.7	84.6	85.7
Plans to shrimp next year			
full-time	07.7	40.0	81.8
part-time	61.5	53.3	09.1
will not shrimp next year	30.8	06.7	09.1
Would like children to shrimp	46.2	53.3	33.3
Under 50 yrs. old	54.5	56.3	59.1
Education			
some college	41.7	25.0	09.1
high school	41.7	18.8	36.4
grade school	16.7	56.3	54.5
Military or trade school	66.7	22.2	28.6
Membership in commer. fishing assoc.	07.7	33.3	72.7
high level of involvement	0.0	06.7	18.2
Membership in community associations	38.5	60.0	45.5
	N=13	N=19	N=19

Notes

PREFACE

1. David R. M. White, "Sea Turtles and Resistance to TEDs among Shrimp Fishermen of the U.S. Gulf Coast." *MAST* 2, no. 1 (1989): 69–79.
2. Karl R. Popper, *The Logic of Scientific Inquiry* (London: Hutchinson, 1969).
3. John Lofland, *Analyzing Social Settings* (Belmont, Calif.: Wadsworth, 1971).

INTRODUCTION

1. The Louisiana Anglers Conservation Association was organized in 1990. LACA grew out of a disgruntled GCCA faction. Some former GCCA members were unhappy with the financial structure of the GCCA and wanted to see more conservation efforts and restrictions placed on commercial harvesters.

2. See Louis A. Helfrich, and Bernard L. Griswold, "Public Education in Fisheries: A Review of the Role of Extension," *Reviews in Aquatic Sciences,* 4 (4), p. 321). About 350 specialists and marine agents are associated with sea-grant institutions nationwide, located in coastal and Great Lake States. The programs they conduct are administered by a national director. Many of the personnel are administratively attached to the Cooperative Extension Service of the U.S. Department of Agriculture but are programmatically responsible to the state sea-grant director. Sea Grant Extension, as does its agricultural counterpart, the Cooperative Extension Service (1) evaluates, synthesizes, and transfers information; (2) facilitates interaction among individuals and groups; (3) stimulates adoption of improved practices; (4) encourages participation in public policy and decision making; and (5) promotes personal development. One could cite a long list of accomplishments credited to Sea Grant programs and marine agents. They have educated the public and user groups, resolved numerous conflicts, developed new aquaculture industries, and have assisted commercial and recreational fishers.

3. The problem of marine debris is, in part, created by the practice of ships dumping garbage overboard before entering port. Of all marine debris sources, plastics are the most durable since they are made from petroleum and are not biodegradable. The Center for Marine Conservation, after citing the economic importance of U.S. shrimp fisheries, "aims to bring new voices into the shrimp

management process." (See Harold F. Upton, Peter Hoar, and Melissa Upton, *The Gulf of Mexico Shrimp Fishery*, p. 2.)

4. The 1993 financial report lists, besides Waste Management Incorporated, American Plastics, Amoco, Chevron, Pepsi-Cola, Shell, Texaco, and about two dozen other corporations.

5. The Magnuson Act was intended to manage and conserve U.S. marine resources. It excluded foreign harvesters from a 200 mile zone surounding the U.S. coast; it restricted U.S. harvesters from fishing within 200 miles of foreign countries; and it created eight regional management councils to advise the Secretary of the Department of Commerce on managing U.S. marine fisheries.

6. In most countries government scientists and/or independent panels make recommendations. This structure does not invite political machinations the way the U.S. Council structure does. For a critical assessment of Council structure, see E. Paul Durrenberger, "Shrimpers and Turtles on the Gulf Coast: The Formation of Fisheries Policy in the United States," MAST 1, no. 2 (1987): 196–214.

7. Louisiana Cooperative Extension Service, *El Pescador* (May 10, 1993).

8. Shrimpers generally believe that pollution can put them out of business. They have participated with environmental groups outside the traditional core environmental movement. Thus, they could be called an opponent group. See Valerie J. Gunter and Barbara Finlay, "Influences on Group Participation in Environmental Conflicts," *Rural Sociology* 53, no. 4 (1988): 504. Some shrimpers believe that their actions as opponents have not been forgotten by some proponents. Shrimpers were part of the grassroots opposition against ocean incineration, a process for which ChemWaste held a permit. In 1986, when the EPA scheduled public hearings at Brownsville, Texas, and Mobile, Alabama, grassroots opposition was intense. The EPA and ChemWaste had to close down incineration operations in the Gulf. A similar fate awaited them on the East Coast at Philadelphia. See Conner Bailey and Charles E. Faupel, "Out of Sight is Not out of Mind: Public Opposition to Ocean Incineration," *Coastal Management* 17, no. 1 (1989): 89–102.

9. In brief, the shrimpers argued that shrimpers collaborated with environmental groups to block ocean incineration; Waste Management Incorporated has given grants to the Center for Marine Conservation, the organization that led the push for TEDS. Waste Management Incorporated has connections with some national environmental groups, and the TEDS regulations were implemented right after EPA withdrew support for ocean incineration. We attempt to evaluate some aspects of this charge in chapter six. Suffice it to say that the national environmental community is divided over the question of accepting funds from corporate polluters. Greenpeace has charged that Waste Management has a notoriously dismal environmental record. See Greenpeace, *An Abstract of Waste Management Inc.: An Encyclopedia of Environmental Crimes and Other Misdeeds* (Chicago: Greenpeace, July, 1990).

CHAPTER 1: TURTLES AND TEDS

1. In order to understand the debate over TEDS and other putative social problems, it is first necessary to examine the two most basic theoretical positions within the literature of social problems. The focus for a theory of social problems is to account for the emergence and maintenance of claims making and responding activities. The theory should address the process by which a putative condition becomes a social problem. See Charles E. Reasons and William D. Perdue, *The Ideology of Social Problems;* Malcolm Spector and John Kitsuse, *Constructing Social Problems*, p. 76; and Steve Woolgar and Dorothy Pawluch, "Ontological Gerrymandering: The Anatomy of Social Problems Explanations," *Social Problems* 32, no. 3 (1985): 214–27.

In the case of the decline of turtles, two scenarios of claims-making activity can explain why it emerged when it did, the traditionalist and the constructionist accounts. The distinctive feature of the social problem argument of the traditionalist is that the undesirable condition has actually increased and, therefore, attention to it has increased. Basically, the constructionist argument is that there has been no significant change in the activity in question, but that activities, or rates of activity, which were not previously defined as problematic, have been defined as a problem. See Herbert Blumer, "Social Problems as Collective Behavior," *Social Problems* 18, no. 3 (1971): 298–306; Lawrence E. Hazelrigg, "Is There a Choice between Constructionism and Objectivism?" *Social Problems* 33, no. 1 (1986): 1–13; and Helen Z. Lopata, "Social Construction of Social Problems over Time," *Social Problems* 31, no. 3 (1984): 249–72.

The reasons for this redefinition are myriad and range from needs for a bureaucracy to maintain clients and vested interest. See Michael Belknap, "The Merchants of Repression," *Crime and Social Justice* 7 (Spring/Summer, 1977): 49–58; Elliott P. Currie, "Crimes without Criminals: Witchcraft and its Control in Renaissance Europe," *Law and Society Review* 6 (1972): 7–32; Donald Dickson, "Bureaucracy and Morality: An Organizational Perspective on a Moral Crusade," *Social Problems* 16, no. 2 (1969): 143–56; Scotty Embree, "The State Department as Moral Entrepreneur: Racism and Imperialism as Factors in the Passage of the Harrison Narcotics Act," in *Corrections and Punishment*, pp. 193–204; Craig Forsyth and Neal Shover. "No Rest for the Weary . . . Constructing a Problem of Elderly Crime," *Sociological Focus* 19, no. 4 (1986): 375–86; Craig Forsyth and Robert Gramling, "Elderly Crime: Fact and Artifact," in *Older Offenders: Perspectives in Criminology and Criminal Justice*, pp. 1–13; Thomas Szasz, *The Manufacture of Madness*, through sensationalism (see J. Best and G. T. Horiuchi, "The Razor Blade in the Apple: The Social Construction of Urban Legends," *Social Problems* 32, no. 5 [1985]: 488–99) to new information (see Craig Forsyth and Marion D. Olivier, "The Theoretical Framing of a Social Problem: Some Conceptual Notes on Satanic Cults," *Deviant Behavior* 11, no. 3

[1990]: 281–92). Whatever the reason, from the constructionist approach, the primary issue is the definition process itself, not the activity. In order to argue the constructionist approach, one must show that the problem has remained relatively constant while interest and concern have increased.

Forsyth and Shover (in "No Rest for the Weary") argue this approach with respect to social problems. They contend that focus on a particular problem is a product of three basic factors. The first of these factors is the vested interest of a bureaucracy. Bureaucracies justify their existence by the number of clients they process. A previously untapped resource becomes a focus.

A second factor is the fashion by which scholarship is evaluated in most academic disciplines. The summa of scholarly activity has always been the publication. Thus, academics are always looking for "hot" new areas of research, where the competition is less fierce and the probability of publication greater.

These two factors are exacerbated by the media. Always hungry for news, the media is all too happy to provide coverage of a new wave (see Mark Fishman, "Crime Waves as Ideology," *Social Problems* 25, no. 5 [1978]: 531–43; Drew Humphries, "Serious Crime, News Coverage, and Ideology: A Content Analysis of Crime Coverage in a Metropolitan Paper," *Crime and Delinquency* 27 [April, 1981]: 191–205; Joseph F. Sheley and Cindy D. Ashkins, "Crime, Crime News, and Crime Views," *Public Opinion Quarterly* 45 [Winter, 1981]: 492–506).

Best and Horiuchi (in "The Razor Blade in the Apple") present a quite similar case. Although the actual incidence of Halloween sadism (putting dangerous objects or substances in children's Halloween candy) has been so consistently low over the last twenty-five years that the probability of a child getting altered candy is virtually zero, the hue and cry fanned by media attention has virtually eliminated trick or treating.

Few social phenomena present themselves in pure black-or-white terms, and the social scientist is generally quite accustomed to working somewhere within the gray spectrum. It is quite unrealistic to expect data to totally support one of the two conceptualizations presented here. Probably the most fruitful way to view the two theoretical positions is as extremes of a continuum. In the case of TEDS, the push to save turtles from shrimpers' trawls began nearly twenty-five years after the Kemp ridleys experienced a dramatic decrease. On the other hand, this timing coincides with increased shrimping effort. Our position is constructionist, but we recognize that a number of objective conditions have changed. It is in this gray area in which most researchers locate emergent social problems. This is where Forsyth and Olivier locate the putative problem of satanic activity, and Forsyth and Gramling explain similar considerations with regard to elderly crime.

2. National Academy of Science, *Decline of the Sea Turtles: Causes and Prevention,* pp. 82–107.

3. Daniel Keith Conner, "Turtles, Trawlers, and TEDS: What Happens When

the Endangered Species Act Conflicts with Fishermen's Interests," *Water Log* 7, no. 4 (1987), pp. 9–10.

4. Ibid.

5. Personal interview, Chuck Oravetz, NMFS, Southeast Region, Office of Protected Species, 1990.

6. Ibid.

7. There is considerable literature on adoption, and a substantial part of it draws upon the experiences of agricultural Extension agents (see Richard T. LaPiere, *Social Change*, pp. 153–55). According to LaPiere (p. 155), agricultural agents have been particularly successful in getting farmers to adopt new seeds, fertlizers, pesticides, etc. by having them attend meetings where they can hear successful adopters praise the new device or practice. This strategy of promotion is based on reference group theory which aspires to create both discontent with old standards of success and the acceptance of new standards. This strategy did not work in the TEDS case, in our opinion, because TEDS came to symbolize everything that was going wrong with shrimping. In any event, outside of our discussion of the difficulties with technical fixes, we chose to avoid the adoption question. We felt strongly that to pose the question would have consumed our energies and set a research agenda we were not disposed to follow. The point is that the researcher asks, "Why didn't the shrimpers adopt TEDS?" At that same moment, the question of whether they should is lost to the research agenda.

8. Personal interviews, Sea Grant Extension gear experts, 1989, 1990.

9. Personal interviews, 1989, 1990.

10. Personal interviews, Sea Grant and NMFS personnel, 1989, 1990.

11. Personal interview, Andy Kemmerer, director, NMFS, Southeast Region, 1990.

12. Conner, "Turtles, Trawlers, and TEDS," p. 11.

13. 52, *Federal Register* 6179, (March 2, 1987).

14. Personal interview, NMFS officials, 1990.

15. *Times-Picayune*, July 22, 1989, pp. F1, F4.

16. We have borrowed this concept of how scientists become partisans in controversies over hazardous wastes. See Pam Scott, Evellen Richards, and Brian Martin, "Captives of Controversy: The Myth of the Neutral Social Researcher in Contemporary Scientific Controversies," *Science Technology and Human Values* 15 (1990): 474–94.

17. Lewis Coser, *The Functions of Social Conflict*, pp. 33–38.

18. M. N. Zald and R. Ash, "Social Movement Organizations," *Social Forces* 44, no. 3 (1966): 327–41.

19. Scott, Richards, and Martin, "Captives of Controversy."

20. Personal interview, Michael Weber, formerly with the Center for Marine Conservation, 1993.

CHAPTER 2: SETTING THE STAGE FOR OIL AND SHRIMP

1. Patricia Marchak, "The Staples Trap," in *Fish vs. Oil*, pp. 178–86.

2. J. D. House, *The Challenge of Oil: Newfoundland's Quest for Controlled Development*; see also House, ed. *Fish vs. Oil*.

3. It was Max Weber's thesis that the Protestant ethic broke down traditionalism and that it was a major factor in the transition from agricultural to industrial society. In *The Protestant Ethic and the Spirit of Capitalism*, (pp. 59–60), Weber gives the following example of traditionalism:

> A man, for instance, who at the rate of 1 mark per acre mowed 2½ acres per day and earned 2½ marks, when the rate raised to 1.25 marks per acre mowed, not 3 acres, as he might easily have done, thus earning 3.75 marks, but only 2 acres, so that he could still earn the 2½ marks to which he was accustomed. The opportunity of earning more was less attractive than that of working less. He did not ask: How much can I earn in a day if I do as much work as possible? but: How much must I do in order to earn the wage 2½ marks, which I earned before and which takes care of my traditional needs? . . . A man does not "by nature" wish to earn more and more money, but simply to live as he is accustomed to live and to earn as much as is necessary to live and for that purpose.

Weber considered such a traditional view to be a hindrance to the development of modern industrial-capitalism. Weber continues, "Wherever modern capitalism has begun its work of increasing its intensity, it has encountered the immensely stubborn resistance of this leading trait of pre-capitalistic labor. And today it encounters it the more, the more backward (from a capitalistic point of view) the laboring forces are with which it has to deal" (ibid., p. 60).

4. R. W. Heber, "Fish and Oil: The Cultural Ecology of Offshore Resource Activities in Nova Scotia," in *Fish vs. Oil*, pp. 162–75.; Marchak, "The Staples Trap."

5. Craig J. Forsyth and DeAnn K. Gauthier, "Families of Offshore Oil Workers: Adaptations to Cyclical Father Absence/Presence," *Sociological Spectrum* 11, no. 2 (1991): 177–201; Robert Gramling, "Concentrated Work Scheduling: Enabling and Constraining Aspects," *Sociological Perspectives* 32, no. 1 (1989): 47–64.

6. Heber, "Fish and Oil."

7. Robert Lee Maril, *Texas Shrimpers: Community, Capitalism, and the Sea.*

8. Robert Gramling, Craig J. Forsyth, and Linda Mooney, "The Protestant Ethic and the Spirit of Cajunism," *Journal of Ethnic Studies* 15, no. 1 (1987): 33–46; H. W. Gilmore, "Social Isolation of the French Speaking People of Rural Louisiana," *Social Forces* 12, no. 1 (1933): 78–84; Vernon J. Parenton, "Notes on

the Social Organization of a French Village in South Louisiana," *Social Forces* 17, no. 1 (1938): 73–82.

9. Gilmore, "Social Isolation"; Parenton, "Notes on Social Organization"; H. W. Gilmore, "Family-Capitalism in a Community of Rural Louisiana," *Social Forces* 15, no. 1 (1936): 71–75; T. Lynn Smith and Vernon J. Parenton, "Acculturation among the Louisiana French," *American Journal of Sociology* 44, no. 3 (1938): 355–64; Clifford Clarke, "Religion and Regional Culture: The Changing Pattern of Religious Affiliation in the Cajun Region of Southwest Louisiana." *Journal for the Scientific Study of Religion* 24, no. 4 (1985): 384–95.

10. Frederick L. Olmstead, *Cotton Kingdom*, pp. 39–40.

11. Smith and Parenton, "Acculturation among the Louisiana French," pp. 356–57.

12. Ibid.

13. Gilmore, "Social Isolation," pp. 79–80.

14. Julian H. Seward, *The Theory Of Cultural Change*. According to Heber ("Fish and Oil," p. 163), "the core or central features of a culture are those that are most closely related to subsistence activities and economic arrangements. Any disruption to the environment that affects these subsistence activities and economic arrangements brings about change to the central features of culture and to the way of life of which they are a part. The consequent social and behavioral changes to a community of people or to a cultural group is the substance of social/economic impact."

15. Gramling, Forsyth, and Mooney, "The Protestant Ethic."

16. M. K. Orbach, *Hunters, Seamen, and Entrepreneurs: The Tuna Seinermen of San Diego;* Jan Horbulewicz, "The Parimeters of the Psychological Autonomy of Industrial Trawler Crews," in *Seafarer and Community,* pp. 67–84.

17. Gramling, "Concentrated Work Scheduling," p. 50.

18. Craig Forsyth and Robert Gramling, "Feast or Famine: Alternative Management Techniques Among Periodic-Father Absence Single Career Families," *International Journal of Sociology of the Family* 17, no. 2 (1987): 183–95.

19. Forsyth and Gauthier, "Families of Offshore Oil Workers"; Robert Gramling and Craig J. Forsyth, "Work Scheduling and Family Interaction," *Journal of Family Issues* 8, no. 2 (1987): 163–75; K. Storey, J. Lewis, M. Shrimpton, and D. Clark, *Family Life Adaptations to Offshore Oil and Gas Employment.*

20. Forsyth and Gauthier, "Families of Offshore Oil Workers," p. 198.

21. Personal interview, shrimper, Morgan City, Louisiana, 1990.

22. Personal interview, shrimper, Cameron, Louisiana, 1990.

23. Personal interview, shrimper, Lafayette, Louisiana, 1990.

24. Personal interview, shrimper, Cameron, Louisiana, 1990.

25. Edward F. Klima, "Approaches to Research and Management of U.S. Fisheries for Penaeid Shrimp in the Gulf of Mexico," in *Offprints from Marine Invertebrate Fisheries: Their Assessment and Management,* pp. 87–113.

26. Offshore fishery accounts for about 70 percent of production (ibid., p. 88).

27. Personal interview, shrimper, Morgan City, Louisiana, 1990.

28. Christopher Dyer and Mark Moberg, "Responses to Forced Innovation: Turtle Excluder Devices (TEDS) and Gulf Coast Fishermen," (paper presented at the American Anthropological Association Meeting, New Orleans, La., 1990) and Stephen Thomas and C. M. Formichella, *The Shrimp Processing Industry in Bayou La Batre, Alabama.*

29. Kathi R. Kitner, *TEDS: A Study of the South Atlantic Shrimp Fishermen's Beliefs, Opinions and Perceptions Regarding the Use of Turtle Excluder Devices.*

30. Susan S. Hanna and Courtland L. Smith, "Attitudes of Trawl Vessel Captains about Work, Resource Use, and Fisheries Management," *North American Journal of Fisheries Management* 13 (1993): 367–75.

31. Maril, *Texas Shrimpers.*

32. Ibid., p. 59.

33. Ibid., pp. 59–60.

34. Ibid., p. 62.

35. Ibid., p. 41.

36. Ibid., p. 113.

37. Orbach, *Hunters, Seamen, and Entrepreneurs*, pp. 272–88; Maril, *Texas Shrimpers*, pp. 75–97.

38. Tunstall, *The Fisherman*, pp. 156–65.

39. Maril, *Texas Shrimpers*; Tunstall, *The Fisherman*, pp. 160–65. Also see R. Anderson, "Hunt and Deceive: Information Management in Newfoundland Deepsea Trawler Fishing," in *North Atlantic Fishermen: Anthropological Essays on Modern Fishing*, pp. 82–97; G. W. Horobin, "Community and Occupation in the Hull Fishing Industry," *British Journal of Sociology* 8, no. 3 (1957): 343–56.; G. Stiles, "Fishermen, Wives, Radios: Aspects of Communication in a Newfoundland Fishing Community," in *North Atlantic Fisherman*, pp. 164–87.

40. Orbach, *Hunters, Seamen, and Entrepreneurs*, p. 281; Tunstall, *The Fisherman*, pp. 176–224; Forsyth and Gauthier, "Families of Offshore Oil Workers," p. 198.

41. Personal interview, shrimper, Morgan City, Louisiana, 1990.

42. Personal interview, shrimper, Patterson, Louisiana, 1990.

43. Personal interview, shrimper, Galveston, Texas, 1990.

44. Forsyth and Gauthier, "Families of Offshore Oil Workers," pp. 177–78.; Gramling, "Concentrated Work Scheduling," pp. 50–51; Robert Gramling and Sarah Brabant, "Boom Towns and Offshore Energy Impact Assessment: The Development of a Comprehensive Model," *Sociological Perspectives* 29, no. 2 (1986): 177–201.

45. Ruth Seydlitz et al., "Development and Social Problems: The Impact of the Offshore Oil Industry on Suicide and Homicide Rates," *Rural Sociology* 58, no. 1, (1993): 101–105.

46. Ottar Brox, *Newfoundland Fishermen in the Age of Industry: A Sociology of Economic Dualism;* William Goode, *World Revolution and Family Patterns,* pp. 10–26; Weber, *The Protestant Ethic,* pp. 47–78.

47. Reginald Byron, "Oil-Related Development in Burra Isle, Shetland," in *Fish vs. Oil,* p. 37.

48. Marchak, "The Staples Trap," pp. 182–184.

49. Ibid, p. 182.

50. Ibid.

51. Personal interview, shrimper, New Iberia, Louisiana, 1990.

CHAPTER 3: BLOCKADES AND PROTESTS

1. Personal interview, Wilma Anderson, former vice president, Concerned Shrimpers of America, 1995.

2. Personal interview, protester, Grande Isle, Louisiana, 1990.

3. Personal interview, Texas fish shed owner, 1990.

4. Personal interview, protester, Aransas, Texas, 1993.

5. *Times-Picayune,* July 4, 1991, p. B5.

6. For a protest action similar to TEDS, see Charles Bisanz, "Brief Communication—The Anatomy of a Mass Public Protest Action: A Shutdown by Independent Truck Drivers," *Human Organizations* 36, no. 1 (1977): 62–66. The behavior of truckers and other protesters is referred to as collective behavior. Numerous scholars have written on the subject (Blumer, "Elementary Collective Groupings"; Denton E. Morrison, "Some Notes toward a Theory on Relative Deprivation, Social Movements, and Social Change," *American Behavioral Scientist* 14, no. 5 [1971]: 675–90; Neil S. Smelser, *Theory of Collective Behavior;* E. Hughes, "Social Changes and Status Protest: An Essay on the Marginal Man," *Phylon* 10 [1949]: 58–65). Protests have also been framed in an assortment of conflict theories (see George Ritzer, *Contemporary Sociological Theory*).

7. Seymour Martin Lipset, *Political Man: The Social Basis of Politics,* pp. 1–24; Howard Kimeldorf's analysis ("Working Class Culture, Occupational Recruitment, and Union Politics," *Social Forces* 64, no. 2 [1985]: 359–76) of the U.S. longshoremen's unions is supportive of Lipset's ideas regarding the roots of extremism. He found that the differences in political radicalism of the two major U.S. longshoremen's unions was shown to be the result of background factors of individuals. ILWU, which is primarily situated on the West Coast, has historically had a political radical left stance because the membership was recruited from nomadic working-class occupations, primarily, seaman, loggers, and fisherman who were either retired or between jobs. The other U.S. longshoremen union (ILA) has been very conservative because the roots of its membership were not the migratory occupations which formed the basis of ILWU membership.

8. Lipset, *Political Man,* pp. 243–44.

9. Lebon, *The Crowd: A Study of the Popular Mind,* pp. 160–65.

10. Blumer, "Elementary Collective Groupings."

11. Smelser, *Theory of Collective Behavior,* pp. 67–78.

12. Morrison, "Some Notes."

13. Robert A. Goldberg, *Grassroots Resistance: Social Movements in Twentieth Century America.*

14. J. Craig Jenkins, "Resource Mobilization Theory and the Study of Social Movements," *Annual Reviews of Sociology* 9 (1983): 52–53.

15. Lipset, *Political Man,* p. 137.

16. Huey Pierce Long served as governor of Louisiana from 1928 to 1932 and was elected senator in 1930. His popular down-home oratorical style and share-the-wealth message during the Depression made him a savior among the masses. His foes countered with labels like "demagogue" and "dictator." His political ambitions, but not his legacy, came to an end in 1935 when he was shot to death in the State Capitol. For an appreciation of the man and his times, see T. Harry Williams, *Huey Long* (New York: Knopf, 1969).

17. Jenkins, "Resource Mobilization Theory."

18. Personal interview, Cajun shrimper, 1990.

19. Personal interview, Vietnamese shrimper, Louisiana, 1990.

20. Personal interview, Louisiana marine agent, 1990.

21. Personal interview, North Carolina shrimper, 1990.

22. Personal interview, Georgia shrimper, 1990.

23. Personal interview, North Carolina shrimper, 1990.

24. Erving Goffman, *The Presentation of Self In Everyday Life,* pp. 70–76.

25. Personal interview, protester at Grande Isle, Louisiana, 1990.

26. Personal interview, Texas marine agent, 1990.

27. Personal interview, Louisiana shrimper, 1990.

28. Personal interview, Georgia marine agent, 1990.

CHAPTER 4: STATES, GOVERNMENT AGENCIES, AND MEDIATION

1. Louisiana's commercial landings (by weight) is second only to Alaska's. Its value also typically exceeds the value of the landings of other states (see National Marine Fisheries, *Fisheries of the United States,* 1989 [Washington, D.C.: U.S. Government Printing Office, 1990], p. 4). The State led the nation in shrimp and oyster production (ibid., p. x).

2. Personal interview, Jerry Clark, Louisiana Wildlife and Fisheries, 1991.

3. *Times-Picayune,* January 29, 1992, B-2.

4. Michael K. Orbach and Jeffrey C. Johnson, "The Transformation of Fishing Communities: A Public Policy Perspective," *Marine Resource Utilization: A*

Conference on Social Science Issues, Mobile University of South Alabama College of Arts and Sciences Publication and the Mississippi-Alabama Sea Grant Consortium 1, no. 1 (1988): 65–70.

5. Senator Bennett Johnston, speech to Concerned Shrimpers of America, Thibodeaux, Louisiana, March 24, 1990.

6. Bills initiated in Congress are often for public relations purposes; nobody really expects them to develop beyond that. The fact that commercial harvesters kept the pressure on Congress to deal with the import problem may have raised some concern in the State Department. Accordingly, the federal government's attempts to mitigate the problems occasioned by the TEDS conflict only widened the circle of conflict.

7. Orbach and Johnson, "The Transformation of Fishing Communities."

8. Personal interview, Ron Becker, Louisiana Sea Grant College Program, 1990.

9. Personal interview, Louisiana marine agent 1, 1990.

10. Personal interview, Texas marine agent, 1990.

11. Personal interview, Louisiana marine agent 2, 1990.

12. Personal interview, Sea Grant official, 1990.

13. Personal interview, Georgia marine agent.

14. Personal interview, Texas marine agent.

15. Personal interview, Mississippi marine agent.

16. Personal interview, Louisiana marine agent.

17. Personal interview, Andy Kemmerer, director, NMFS, Southeast Region, 1990.

18. Personal interview, Ralph Rayburn, former director, Texas Shrimp Association, 1991.

19. Ibid.

20. Personal interview, Andy Kemmerer, 1990.

21. Personal interview, Wilma Anderson, TSA board member and former vice president, Concerned Shrimpers of America, 1990.

22. Personal interview, Deyaun Boudreaux, TSA board, 1990.

23. Personal interview, Leonard Crosby, Georgia shrimper, 1990.

24. Personal interview, Michael Weber, Center for Marine Conservation, 1993.

25. The structure and function of the Councils is defined by the Magnuson Act of 1976 and has been criticized harshly (see Durrenberger, "Shrimpers and Turtles on the Gulf Coast," pp. 196–214). The Councils' appointment process is a product of political compromises. All the councils have the same general structure and mandate. There is, however, considerable variation in the way each regional council functions.

In an attempt to be better informed on the social and economic impacts of fishery plans, the Gulf Council created the Socioeconomic Assessment Panel (SEP). The SEP is charged with informing the Council on social and economic impacts regulations will have on fisheries in a way that parallels the role of the Stock Assessment Panel's (SAP) advice on stock assessments. It is presently working toward greater coordination and exploring ways to make the SEP's data and analyses comparable to the data and analyses generated by the SAP. Unfortunately, very little progress has been made so far. The major source of data the SEP uses in its deliberations comes from the Southeast Office of NMFS, which has been woefully inadequate in performing its charge. Citing budgetary restraints and personnel limitations, NMFS recognizes the inadequacies.

26. We draw upon Quadagno's state transformation theory to focus our discussion; see Jill Quadagno, "Social Movements and State Transformation: Labor and Racial Conflict in the War on Poverty," *American Sociological Review* 57, no. 5 (1992): 630–32. State transformation theory (1) emphasizes a "dialectical interaction between the state and societal factors", (2) argues that "state policies shape the definitions of ideological issues", (3) hypothesizes that the "permeability of state agencies to social movement demands depends on their autonomy from the targets of social movement goals", and (4) contends that the "structural and ideological gains represent real gains, not merely the co-optation of social movement activists and goals."

27. Quadagno, "Social Movements and State Transformation," pp. 628–32.

28. Ibid., pp. 630–32.

29. A great deal has been written and debated on the relative autonomy of the state. This note serves as a brief summary of that debate. Historically, the capitalist state has had to perform two opposing functions (see Craig Forsyth, "Economic Infrastructures and the Development of State Autonomy: A Case Study of U.S. Maritime Policy," *Sociological Spectrum* 8, no. 4 [1988]: 303–22; Craig Forsyth, *The American Merchant Seaman,* pp. 2–3; J. O'Connor, *The Fiscal Crisis of the State,* pp. 7–9). The state must always function to allow capital accumulation and at the same time to preserve its own legitimacy (see Claus Offe, "The Abolition of Market Control and the Problem of Legitimacy," *Kapitalistate* 1, no. 2 [1973]: 109–16). "It must simultaneously be a class state and a universal state" (see Alan Wolfe, "New Directions in the Marxist Theory of Politics," *Politics and Society* 4 [1974], p. 149; Bob Jessop, "On Recent Marxist Theories of Law, the State, and Juridio-Political Ideology," *International Journal of the Sociology of Law* 8, no. 3 [1980]: 339–68).

The relationship between the state and the dominant class is necessitated by the fact that the state is immediately dependent on the economy. State managers cannot ignore the necessity of assisting the process of capital accumulation; this would risk drying up the source of state power: the economy's surplus production capacity, and the taxes drawn from this surplus and other forms of capital. But the capitalist state that openly uses its coercive force to help one class accumulate capital at the expense of other classes may lose its legitimacy and hence undermine the basis of its support and loyalty (see O'Connor, *The Fiscal*

Crisis of the State, p. 8). The legitimacy of the state is further contingent upon a healthy economy, since all citizens hold the state accountable for their economic well-being (see David Butler and Donald Stokes, *Political Change in Britain*). Hence, state managers must serve accumulation and legitimacy and mediate the conflict that is inherent in these contradictory functions. The capitalist state also has emergent interests.

This goes beyond the conventional neo-Marxian notion of relative autonomy that is required to mediate the conflict resulting from the capitalist system (see O'Connor, *The Fiscal Crisis of the State;* Wolfe, "New Directions", pp. 135–37; Nicos Poulantzas, *Political Power and Social Classes*, pp. 285–86). These interests are more consistent with a neo-Weberian theory of political economy which views the state as an organization serving its own needs for growth, sustenance, and legitimacy (see Stephen J. McNamee, "DuPont-State Relations," *Social Problems* 34, no. 1 [1987]: 1–17; Frank Hearn, "State Autonomy and Capitalism," *Contemporary Crisis* 8, no. 2 [1984]: 125–45). The key characteristic of the state, from a neo-Weberian perspective, is its reproductive character: the ability to keep itself in existence (see Wolfe, "New Directions," p. 135; Louis Althusser, *For Marx*). These interests, particularly as they involve enhanced strength and autonomy, are most palpable during periods of crisis (see John L. Campbell, "The State and the Nuclear Waste Crisis: An Institutional Analysis of Policy Constraints," *Social Problems* 34, no. 1 [1987]: 18–33).

In these situations state managers act contrary to the preferences of the dominant class in order to ensure state autonomy and survival. During these periods state managers make reforms in the name of mollifying pressures from below, but shape these concessions so as to enhance state power and the role of the state in the economy. In time this increased power of the state gains acceptance from the capitalist class because these reforms become recognized as essential to the objectives of capitalism (see Hearn, "State Autonomy and Capitalism," pp. 129–30). Gradually, the process of capital accumulation becomes dependent upon and contoured by state policy.

In advanced capitalism state managers set the rules for most economic transactions, directly regulate the class struggle through labor laws, determine the size of the social wage, provide the infrastructure of capital accumulation, manage economic growth and the tempo of business activity, take measures directly and indirectly to maintain effective demand, and have the state participate in the market as a massive business actor and employer (see Karl Klare, "Law-Making as Praxis," *Telos* 12, no. 2 [1979], p. 125).

CHAPTER 5: SCIENCE AND MAGIC

1. The idea that science is socially constructed is the theme of Kuhn's classic work (Thomas S. Kuhn, *The Structure of Scientific Revolutions*, p. 126):

Are theories simply man-made interpretations of given data? The episte-
mological viewpoint that has guided Western Philosophy for three cen-
turies dictates an immediate and equivocal Yes! . . . The operations and
measurements that a scientist undertakes in the laboratory are not the
given of experience but rather "the collected with difficulty." They are
not what the scientist sees—at least not before his research is well advanced and his attention focused. Rather they are concrete indices to the
content of more elementary perceptions, and as such they are selected
for close scrutiny of normal research only because they promise opportunity for the fruitful elaboration of an accepted paradigm.

2. Pitirim A. Sorokin, *Society, Culture, and Personality,* pp. 607–19.

3. T. A. Henwood and W. E. Stuntz, "Analysis of Sea Turtle Captures and
Mortalities during Commercial Shrimp Trawling," *Fisheries Bulletin* 85 (1987):
813–17.

4. National Academy of Science, *Decline of the Sea Turtles,* pp. 97–100.

5. Ibid.

6. Frank Schwartz, correspondence to Nancy Foster, NMFS national office,
July 23, 1990.

7. Ibid.

8. Nicholas A. Ashford, "Science and Values in the Regulatory Process."
Statistical Science 3, no. 3 (1988): 377–83.

9. Ibid., p. 379.

10. Ibid. Statisticians should recognize the two errors that are the horns of the
bull in Ashford's dilemma: accepting the null when it is false and rejecting the
null when it is true.

11. The TEDS Observer Program was mandated by the Office of Management
and Budget. Shrimpers used a trawl with a TED on one side and another trawl
without a TED (see Maurice Renaud et al., *Evaluations of the Impacts of TEDs,*
NOAA Technical Memo NMFSSEFC-254, 1990).

12. Authors' notes taken at the CSA Board meeting, Kenner, Louisiana, 1990.

13. Personal interview, Michael Bean, signatory to the TEDS agreement, 1990.

14. Marydale Donnelly of the Center for Marine Conservation was commented to the newspaper (see *Times-Picayune,* September 1, 1991, B1,2) on turtle
nestings. The two years of TEDS use that she links with the increase in nestings
were years of very low compliance.

15. Personal interview, Louisiana marine agent, 1990.

16. Personal interview, Georgia marine agent, 1990.

17. Personal interview, Andy Kemmerer, Southeast Region director, October,
1990.

18. Personal interview, Rick Condry, Louisiana State University Sea Grant, 1990.

19. TEDS Observer Program, 1990.

20. Personal interview, Louisiana environmentalist, 1990.

21. Personal interview, Suzanne Montero, NMFS law enforcement director, 1990.

CHAPTER 6: THE ENVIRONMENTALISTS' CHALLENGE

1. Personal interview, Wilma Anderson, board member of Texas Shrimp Association and former vice president of Concerned Shrimpers, 1990.

2. Personal interview, Deyaun Boudreaux, board member of the Texas Shrimp Association, 1990.

3. Authors' notes, Gulf of Mexico Fishery Management Council Meeting, New Orleans, Louisiana, September, 1990.

4. Personal interview, Michael Weber, 1993.

5. Personal interview, Vance Hughes, signatory of the TEDS agreement, 1990.

6. We have constructed this brief history of turtle protection from several interviews of environmentalists and government officials: David Cottingham, NOAA, Office of the Chief Scientist, October 18, 1990; Chuck Oravitz, NMFS Office of Protected Species, Southeast Region office, October 26, 1990; William Siddal, gear specialist, NMFS Laboratory, Pascagoula, Mississippi, June 18, 1991; Michael Weber, former vice president for programs, Center for Marine Conservation, October 16, 1990; Michael Bean, environmental lawyer, Environmental Defense Fund, October 18, 1990. These interviews covered topics related to the TEDS conflict, not just turtle listings.

7. Personal interview, Michael Weber, Center for Marine Conservation and signatory of the TEDS agreement, 1993.

8. Personal interview, Michael Weber, 1993. For a discussion of philanthropy in general, see David M. Ermann, "The Operative Goals of Corporate Philanthropy: Contributions to the Public Broadcasting Service, 1972–1976," *Social Problems* 25, no. 3 (1978): 504–14; David M. Ermann and Richard J. Lundman, *Corporate Deviance;* Irwin Ross, "Public Relations Isn't Kid Stuff at Mobil," *Fortune* 94 (September, 1976), p. 10.

9. Warren T. Brookes, *Conservative Chronicle*, June 26, 1991, p. 5.

10. Ibid., p. 15.

11. *Times-Picayune*, August 18, 1991, pp. F1, F4. A distinction should be made between ocean dumping and ocean incineration. Some suspect that Waste Management has fought ocean dumping because its landfills would do more business. Ocean incineration, however, was intended to dispose of hazardous wastes and would have been a very profitable venture were it not for the strong opposition from the public and some environmental groups.

12. Ibid.

13. Personal interview, Brian Lipset, Citizens Clearinghouse for Toxic Wastes, Arlington, Virginia, August 29, 1990. Our own records for 1987 and 1988 (second

quarter) show grants of $20,000 and $25,000 respectively awarded to the Center for Environmental Education [CMC] for work on ocean dumping. The Center for Marine Conservation's Financial Statement for 1993 lists as major contributers, among others, Waste Management Incorporated, the Society of the Plastics Industry, American Plastics Council, and major oil companies. Government agencies listed included NOAA, NMFS, and Texas Parks and Wildlife. For a discussion of grassroots groups' sensitivity to environmental justice questions, see Andrew Szasz, *Ecopopulism: Toxic Wastes and Movements for Environmental Justice*, pp. 150–61.

14. Personal interview, Lipset, 1990.

15. *Times Picayune*, 1991.

16. Although we are not claiming that local chapters did not support their national environmental headquarters, we do feel that local groups often have different priorities. A good example is the protest of the Formosa plant in Calhoun County, Texas. Mialjevitch and protesting shrimpers, together with a number of local environmental groups, protested the failure of government to check pollution from the plant. Besides a number of local environmental groups, Coastal Bend Sierra Club was represented. Diane Wilson, president of Calhoun County Resource, organized the protest. She argued that "industrial pollution is a greater threat to sea turtle survival than shrimpers' trawls." By contrast, Elaine Giessel, president of Coastal Bend Sierra Club, supported the protest against Formosa and made it clear that her support of the protest did not mean the Sierra Club supported the ban on TEDS. See Paul Fortney, editorial, *Port Lavaca Wave*, July 1, 1991, pp. 1–2.

17. Personal interviews, former president of local Sierra Club chapter, 1991, 1993.

18. Personal interview, Texas environmentalist, 1990.

19. Our analysis is largely based on the Weber-Michels theory of organizational change, as modified by Zald and Ash (see M. N. Zald, and R. Ash, "Social Movement Organizations," *Social Forces* 44, no. 3 [1966]: 327–41) and augmented by the resource mobilization theory of McCarthy and Zald (see John McCarthy and Mayer N. Zald, "Resource Mobilization and Social Movements: A Partial Theory," *American Journal of Sociology* 82, no. 5 [1977]: 1214–16). Briefly, main points and assumptions of these theories are: (1) the environmental movement is embodied in a large number of movement organizations that differ in both goals and structure; (2) initially, the movement met with some resistance from the public and policymakers; (3) eventually some of the movement's ideals won acceptance; (4) organizations within the movement vary in the type of goals and tactics they prescribe, group structure, and level of success; (5) goals and tactics may vary from radical to conservative; group structure may vary from democratic and unstructured types to bureaucratically structured types; (6) success is often accompanied with increasing bureaucracy and more conservative goals; (7) successful bureaucratic organizations are more likely to compromise on

some of their original goals and may also become more interested in survival and continuing success than pursuing their original mission; (8) all organizations even when they pursue similar goals compete for limited resources; and (9) resources include members, public opinion, finances, knowledge and information, and influence among policymakers.

CHAPTER 7: LEISURE AND COASTAL DEVELOPMENT

1. Personal interview, Deyaun Boudreaux, TSA board member, 1990.

2. Personal interview, Wilma Anderson, TSA board member, 1990.

3. Kathi R. Kitner, TEDs: A Study of the South Atlantic Shrimp Fishermen's Beliefs, Opinions, and Perceptions regarding the Use of Turtle Excluder Devices, Technical Report 5. Charleston, S.C.: South Atlantic Fishery Management Council, 1987.

4. Trellis G. Green and Edward Nissan, "Economic Analysis for Resolving Disputes between Commercial and Recreational Fisheries," Conference on Gulf and South Atlantic Fisheries: Law and Policy, New Orleans, La.: March 18–20, 1987, Louisiana Sea Grant and Mississippi-Alabama Sea Grant Consortium.

5. Personal communication with members of the Florida Fisheries Commission, September, 1990.

6. In fact resident elites in Florida do try to curb development. The conflict between preserving environmental amenities and land development is causing many to rethink their pro-growth stance.

7. Personal interview, an environmental lawyer, Washington, D.C., 1990.

8. Personal interview, a Louisiana lawyer and GCCA member, 1990.

9. Authors' notes on speech by Bob Jones, president of Southeast Fisheries Association, presented at the thirty-first annual meeting of the Louisiana Shrimp Association, March 2–3, 1990.

10. Personal interview, Donald Lirette, president, Terrebonne Fishermen's Organization, 1991.

11. Personal interview, Mississippi marine agent, 1990.

12. Personal interview, Louisiana marine agent, 1990.

13. Personal interview, Texas marine agent, 1990.

14. John R. Logan and Harvey L. Molotch, Urban Fortunes: The Political Economy of Place (Berkeley: University of California Press, 1987), pp. 50–98.

15. Ibid. pp. 50–84.

16. Ibid. pp. 85–98.

17. Modernization theory assumes that (1) a series of evolutionary stages from undeveloped to developed occur during economic development; (2) internal differences among societies are responsible for variations in the rate of development; (3) these internal differences are both structural and social-psychological; (4) modernization is quickened when less developed societies make frequent

contact with developed ones; and (5) economic and technological aid to less developed nations hastens modernization (see Talcott Parsons, *Societies: Evolutionary and Comparative Perspectives*, pp. 21–29; E. E. Hagen, *On the Theory of Social Change*; Alex Inkeles, "The Modernization of Man in Socialist and Nonsocialist Countries," in *Social Consequences of Modernization in Communist Societies*, pp. 50–59; W. W. Rostow, *The Stages of Economic Growth: A Non-Communist Manifesto*).

Challenging modernization theory, a number of writers have argued that the relationship between developed and less developed nations has been exploitative and that the developed nations receive far more than they give. A relevant example is the development of fisheries in third world countries. Multilateral and bilateral aid to third world countries has benefitted foreign donors and native urban elites to the detriment of indigeneous fishers and the fishery stocks. See Conner Bailey "The Political Economy of Fisheries Development," *Agriculture & Human Values* V [1988], pp. 35–48. (For a general discussion see Samir Amin, *Accumulation on a World Scale*; Arghiri Emmanuel, *Unequal Exchange: A Study of the Imperialism of Trade*; Andre Gunder Frank, *Latin America: Underdevelopment or Revolution*; Andre Gunder Frank, "The Development of Underdevelopment," in *Imperialism and Underdevelopment: A Reader*, pp. 4–17). Dependency further widens the gap between the developed and the developing nations. Dependency theory's focus, therefore, is the unequal exchange between nations. However, the multilateral and global context of relationships among nations compels a worldwide focus.

Wallerstein extends dependency theory to incorporate a world-system of nations. Accordingly, each nation is part of a world-system of labor division and stratification (see Immanuel Wallerstein, *The Modern World-System: Capitalist Agriculture and the Origins of the European World-Economy in the Sixteenth Century*).

The empirical and theoretical weaknesses of dependency theory and world-system theory have already been addressed by a number of writers (see Robert Brenner, "The Origins of Capitalist Development: A Critique of Neo-Smithian Marxism," *New Left Review* 104, no. 1 [1977]: 25–92; Daniel Chirot and Thomas D. Hall, "World-System Theory," *Annual Review of Sociology* 8, no. 1 [1982]: 92–93; Susan A. Mann, "The Rise of Wage Labor in the Cotton South: A Global Analysis," *Journal of Peasant Studies* 14, no. 2 [1987]: 226–42). However, despite their weaknesses, dependency and world-system theories are useful to explain "backwardness" as a product of unequal relations among nations. The unequal exchanges between developed and less developed nations are acted out in the economic and political spheres as dominant-subordinate relations. The developed countries exert political influence and receive economic benefits to the detriment of the less developed nations (see Terry Boswell and William J. Dixon, "Dependency and Rebellion: A Cross-National Analysis," *American Sociological*

Review 55, no. 4 [1990]: 540–59; Walter Gillis Peacock, Greg A. Hoover, and Charles D. Killian, "Divergence and Convergence in International Development: A Decomposition Analysis of Inequality in the World System," *American Sociological Review* 53, no. 6 [1988]: 838–52).

18. Pope John XXIII, *Mater Et Magistra: Christianity and Social Progress,* p. 48.

19. Uneven development within nations has been the major concern of dual economy theory. Dual economy theory arose out of the social policy issues of the 1960s, particularly the persistence of poverty and the perceived deterioration of the work environment (see Randy Hodson and Robert L. Kaufman, "Economic Dualism: A Critical Review," *American Sociological Review* 47, no. 6 [1982]: 727–39). By highlighting the "importance of the organization of capital as a factor conditioning workplace outcomes" and the specification of dependency between "core" and "periphery" (ibid., p. 735), the dual economy theory logically extended the dependency theory. Additionally, other theoretical approaches to the dominant-subordinate relations within societies have also been employed.

Dependency of one region or sector on another in the United States has been chronicled by a score of writers (see Susan Mann and James M. Dickerson, "Obstacles to the Development of Capitalist Agriculture," *Journal of Peasant Studies* 5, no. 4 [1978]: 466–81; Harry M. Caudill, *Night Comes to the Cumberlands: A Biography of a Depressed Area;* James C. Cobb, *Industrialization and Southern Society 1877–1984*). Mann and Dickerson see the area west of the Mississippi in the late nineteenth century as an example of "settler internal colonialism." During this period, Indians were forcefully removed and their lands were expropriated. While the forced removal of colonized people is largely a nineteenth century phenomenon, the nineteenth and twentieth century South has also been in a dependent relationship with northern centers of manufacturing and finance (see Cobb, *Industrialization and Southern Society 1877–1984;* Richard A. Couto, "TVA, Appalachian Underdevelopment, and the Post-Industrial Era," *Sociological Spectrum* 8, no. 4 [1988]: 323–48).

20. Cobb, *Industrialization and Southern Society 1877–1984,* pp. 121–35.

21. Ibid, pp. 25–26.

22. William Cronon, *Nature's Metropolis: Chicago and the Great West.*

23. Amos Hawley, *Urban Studies: An Ecological Approach,* p. 220.

24. Craig J. Forsyth and Thomas Marckese, "Thrills and Skills: A Sociological Analysis of Poaching," *Deviant Behavior* 14, no. 2 (1993): 157–72.

25. Hodson and Kaufman, "Economic Dualism," p. 727.

26. *State Times,* February 22, 1991, p. B6.

27. Peter R. Sinclair, "Fisheries and Regional Development: Contradictions of Canadian policy in the Newfoundland Context," *Proceedings of Marine Resource Utilization: A Conference on Social Science Issues,* Mobile, Alabama: University of South Alabama Publication Service, 1988.

28. Orbach and Johnson, "The Transformation of Fishing Communities," pp. 65–70.

29. Dennis E. Gale and Suzanne Hart. "Who Supports State-Sponsored Growth Management Programs? Insights From Maine" (paper presented at the annual meeting of the Association of Collegiate Schools of Planning, Austin, Tex., 1990); Daphne Spain, "Been Heres vs. Come Heres: A Theory of Community Change" (paper presented at the annual meeting of the Association of Collegiate Schools of Planning, Austin, Tex., 1990).

30. Spain, "Been Heres vs. Come Heres", pp. 13–14; Gale and Hart, "Who Supports?", pp. 6–9.

31. Ibid.

32. Spain, "Been Heres vs. Come Heres," p. 14.

33. Ibid., p. 13.

34. Gale and Hart, "Who Supports?" p. 7.

35. The collision between gambling and tourists interests has been brewing for some time. With continued delays on the New Orleans scene, investors were encouraged to locate their casinos on the Mississippi Gulf Coast. In August, 1993, an agreement was finally reached between the two casino groups (*Times-Picayune*, August 23, 1993, p. 1).

36. *Times-Picayune*, June 7, 1992, p. B2.

37. The Tampa sponge fishery is an example of a fishery preserved for tourists. Other examples can be found on the Pacific coast.

CHAPTER 8: LAWS, CONFLICT, AND ORGANIZATIONAL RESPONSE

1. Raymond J. Michalowski and Ronald C. Kramer. "The Space between Laws: The Problem of Corporate Crime in a Transnational Context," *Social Problems* 34, no. 1 (1987): 34–53.

2. Stephen Fox, *John Muir and His Legacy: The American Conservation Movement*, pp. 333–57.

3. Ibid.

4. R. E. Dunlap and K. D. Van Liere, "Commitment to the Dominant Social Paradigm and Concern for Environment Quality," *Social Science Quarterly* 65, no. 4 (1984): 1010–28.

5. One could say that the two conflicting issues are at the core of environmental debates. Either nature has an intrinsic value apart from its use value or it does not. Preservationists believe that nature has an intrinsic value. Conservationists, by contrast, believe that the value of nature stems from its human use value.

6. Ermann and Lundman, *Corporate Deviance*, pp. 98–100.

7. U.S. Code Public Law 93-205; Steven Lewis Yaffee, *Prohibitive Policy: Implementing the Federal Endangered Species Act.*

8. U.S. Code Public Law 16: 1539.

9. Ibid., p. 1532.

10. U.S. Code Public Law 100-240: 2701–2702.

11. Yaffee, *Prohibitive Policy*, p. 165.

12. U.S. Code PL 94-265.

13. N. P. Reed and D. Drabelle, *The United States Fish and Wildlife Service*, p. 12.

14. Senate Report No. 100-240, 2702.

15. Morton Miller, Paul J. Hooker, and Peter H. Fricke. "Impressions of Ocean Fisheries Management under the Magnuson Act," (paper presented at the annual meeting of the American Association for the Advancement of Science, New Orleans, Louisiana, Feb. 17, 1990).

16. Personal interview, Andy Kemmerer, director, NMFS Southeast Region, 1990.

17. Personal interview, Edward Klima, director, NMFS Galveston lab, 1990.

18. Personal interview, Wilma Anderson, 1992.

APPENDIX

1. For a discussion of estimating variance for stratified samples, see Leslie Kish, Survey Sampling.

2. Personal interview, staff members, NMFS southeast office, 1991.

3. Personal interview, Louisiana Wildlife and Fisheries official, 1991.

4. Baron-Mounce, Keithly, and Roberts, Shrimp Facts, pp. 1–19.

5. Kathi R. Kitner, TEDs: A Study of the South Atlantic Shrimp Fishermen's Beliefs, Opinions and Perceptions Regarding the Use of Turtle Excluder Devices.

6. Dunlap and Van Liere, "Dominant Social Paradigm," pp. 1010–28.

7. Baron-Mounce, Keithly, and Roberts, Shrimp Facts, pp. 18–19, reports on the participation in the Louisiana shrimp fishery. However, this a summary document and does not contain a discussion of sample estimates. We have discussed the authors sampling procedure and estimates with Walter Keithly and conclude that our estimates are comparable to theirs.

8. Ibid.

9. Ibid.

Bibliography

Althusser, Louis. *For Marx*. New York: Pantheon, 1970.

Amin, Samir. *Accumulation on a World Scale*. New York: Monthly Review Press, 1978.

Anderson, Lee G. "A Management Agency Perspective of the Economics of Fisheries Regulation." *Marine Resource Economics* 4, no. 2 (1987): 123–31.

———. "Uncertainty in the Fisheries Management Process." *Marine Resource Economics* 1, no. 1 (1984): 77–87.

Anderson, R. "Hunt and Deceive: Information Management in Newfoundland Deepsea Trawler Fishing." In *North Atlantic Fishermen: Anthropological Essays on Modern Fishing*, edited by R. Anderson and C. Wadel. Toronto: University of Toronto Press, 1972.

Ashford, Nicholas A. "Science and Values in the Regulatory Process." *Statistical Science* 3, no. 3 (1988): 377–83.

Babbie, Earl. *The Practice of Social Research*. Belmont, Calif.: Wadworth. 1992.

Bailey, Conner. "The Political Economy of Fisheries Development in the Third World." *Agriculture and Human Values* 5 (1988): 35–48.

Bailey, Conner, and Charles E. Faupel. "Out of Sight Is Not out of Mind: Public Opposition to Ocean Incineration." *Coastal Management* 17, no. 1 (1989): 89–102.

Baron-Mounce, Elizabeth; Walter Keithly; and Kenneth J. Roberts. *Shrimp Facts*. Baton Rouge: Louisiana Sea Grant College Program, 1991.

Belknap, Michael. "The Merchants of Repression." *Crime and Social Justice* 7 (Spring/Summer, 1977): 49–58.

Bell, Daniel. *The End Of Ideology*. New York: Free Press, 1960.

Best, J., and G. T. Horiuchi. "The Razor Blade in the Apple: The Social Construction of Urban Legends." *Social Problems* 32, no. 5 (1985): 488–99.

Bisanz, Charles F. "Brief Communication—The Anatomy of a Mass Public Protest Action: A Shutdown by Independent Truck Drivers." *Human Organization* 36, no. 1 (1977): 62–66.

Blauner, Robert. *Racial Oppression in America*. New York: Harper and Row, 1972.

———. "Internal Colonialism and Ghetto Revolt." *Social Problems* 16, no. 3 (1969): 393–408.

Blumer, Herbert. "Elementary Collective Groupings." In *Principles of Sociology,* edited by Alfred McClung. New York: Barnes and Noble, Inc., 1969.

———. "Social Problems as Collective Behavior." *Social Problems* 18, no. 3 (1971): 298–306.

Boswell, Terry, and William J. Dixon. "Dependency and Rebellion: A Cross-National Analysis." *American Sociological Review* 55, no. 4 (1990): 540–59.

Brabant, Sarah; Craig J. Forsyth; and Robert Gramling. "Organizational Change in the Roman Catholic Church: The Marriage Preparation Policy as Case Study." *Review of Religious Research* 33, no. 3 (1992): 256–69.

Brenner, Robert. "The Origins of Capitalist Development: A Critique of Neo-Smithian Marxism." *New Left Review* 104, no. 1 (1977): 25–92.

Browne, William P. "Mobilizing and Activating Group Demands: The American Agriculture Movement. *Social Science Quarterly* 64, no. 1 (1983): 19–34.

Brox, Ottar. *Newfoundland Fishermen in the Age of Industry: A Sociology of Economic Dualism.* St. John's, Newfoundland: Institute of Social and Economic Research, Memorial University, 1972.

Bryant, Clinton D. "The Zoological Connection: Animal Related Human Behavior." *Social Forces* 58, no. 2 (1979): 399–421.

Butler, David, and Donald Stokes. *Political Change in Britain.* New York: St. Martin's Press, 1974.

Byron, Reginald. "Oil-Related Development in Burra Isle, Shetland." In *Fish vs. Oil,* edited by J. D. House. St. John's, Newfoundland: Institute of Social and Economic Research, Memorial University, 1986.

Campbell, John L. "The State and the Nuclear Waste Crisis: An Institutional Analysis of Policy Constraints." *Social Problems* 34, no. 1 (1987): 18–33.

Caudill, Harry M. *Night Comes to the Cumberlands: A Biography of a Depressed Area.* Boston: Little, Brown and Co., 1962.

Charles, Anthony T. "Fishery Socioeconomics: A Survey." *Land Economics* 64, no. 3 (1988): 276–95.

Chirot, Daniel, and Thomas D. Hall. "World-System Theory." *Annual Review of Sociology* 8, no. 1 (1982): 81–106.

Clarke, Clifford. "Religion and Regional Culture: The Changing Pattern of Religious Affiliation in the Cajun Region of Southwest Louisiana." *Journal for the Scientific Study of Religion* 24, no. 4 (1985): 384–95.

Cobb, James C. *Industrialization and Southern Society 1877–1984.* Lexington: University of Kentucky Press, 1984.

Conner, Daniel Keith. "Turtles, Trawlers, and TEDS: What Happens When the Endangered Species Act Conflicts with Fishermen's Interests." *Water Log: A Legal Reporter of the Mississippi-Alabama Sea Grant Consortium* 7, no. 4 (1987): 3–35.

Cooper, Christopher. "Gulf Shrimpers Attack TEDS." *National Fisherman* (October, 1989): 2–4, 67.

Coser, Lewis. *The Functions Of Social Conflict.* New York: Free Press, 1956.

Couto, Richard A. "TVA, Appalachian Underdevelopment, and the Post-Industrial Era." *Sociological Spectrum* 8, no. 4 (1988): 323–48.

Coyer, Brian Wilson, and Don S. Schwerin. "Bureaucratic Regulation and Farmer Protest in the Michigan PCB Contamination Case." *Rural Sociology* 46, no. 4 (1981): 703–23.

Cronon, William. *Nature's Metropolis: Chicago and the Great West.* New York: Norton, 1991.

Currie, Elliott P. "Crimes without Criminals: Witchcraft and Its Control in Renaissance Europe." *Law and Society Review* 6, no. 1 (1972): 7–32.

Devine, Joel. "Fiscal Policy and Class Income Inequality: The Distributional Consequences of Governmental Revenues and Expenditures in the United States, 1949–1976." *American Sociological Review* 48, no. 5 (1983): 606–22.

Dickson, Donald. "Bureaucracy and Morality: An Organizational Perspective on a Moral Crusade." *Social Problems* 16, no. 2 (1969): 143–56.

Domhoff, G. William. *Who Rules America Now?* Englewood Cliffs, N.J.: Prentice Hall, 1983.

Dunlap, R. E., and K. D. Van Liere. "Commitment to the Dominant Social Paradigm and Concern for Environment Quality." *Social Science Quarterly* 65, no. 4 (1984): 1010–28.

Durrenberger, E. Paul. "Shrimpers and Turtles on the Gulf Coast: The Formation of Fisheries Policy in the United States." *MAST* 1, no. 2 (1987): 196–214.

Dyer, Christopher, and Mark Moberg. "Responses to Forced Innovation: Turtle Excluder Devices (TEDS) and Gulf Coast Fishermen." Paper presented at the American Anthropological Association Meeting, New Orleans, Louisiana, 1990.

Eitzen, D. Stanley. *In Conflict and Order: Understanding Society.* Boston: Allyn and Bacon, 1982.

Embree, Scotty. "The State Department as Moral Entrepreneur: Racism and Imperialism as Factors in the Passage of the Harrison Narcotics Act." In *Corrections and Punishment,* edited by David F. Greenberg. Beverly Hills: Sage Publications, 1977.

Emmanuel, Arghiri. *Unequal Exchange: A Study of the Imperialism of Trade.* New York: Monthly Review Press, 1972.

Endangered Species Act, USCS 16: 1539.

Ermann, M. David. "The Operative Goals of Corporate Philanthropy: Contributions to the Public Broasting Service, 1972–1976. *Social Problems* 25, no. 3 (1978): 504–14.

Ermann, M. David, and Richard J. Lundman. *Corporate Deviance.* New York: Holt, Rinehart and Winston, 1982.

Evans, William. "Fisheries Legislative Initiatives for the 100th Congress." *Proceeding of the Conference on Gulf and South Atlantic Fisheries: Law and Policy.* University of Mississippi Coastal and Marine Law Research Program, Law Center, Mississippi State University, 1987.

Federal Register (52 Fed. Reg 6179, March 2, 1987).

Fishery Conservation, USCS 16: 1852.

Fishman, Mark. "Crime Waves as Ideology." *Social Problems* 25, no. 5 (1978): 531–43.

Forsyth, Craig. *The American Merchant Seaman and His Industry: Struggle and Stigma.* New York: Taylor and Francis, 1989.

———. "Determinants of Family Integration among Merchant Seamen." *International Journal of Sociology of the Family* 18, no. 1 (1988): 33–44.

———. "Economic Infrastructures and the Development of State Autonomy: A Case Study of U.S. Maritime Policy." *Sociological Spectrum* 8, no. 4 (1988): 303–22.

Forsyth, Craig J., and DeAnn K. Gauthier. "Families of Offshore Oil Workers: Adaptations to Cyclical Father Absence/Presence." *Sociological Spectrum* 11, no. 2 (1991): 177–201.

Forsyth, Craig, and Robert Gramling. "Adaptive Familial Strategies among Merchant Seamen." *Lifestyles: Family and Economic Issues* 11, no. 2 (1990): 183–98.

———. "Elderly Crime: Fact and Artifact." In *Older Offenders: Perspectives in Criminology and Criminal Justice,* edited by B. R. McCarthy and R. Langworthy. New York: Praeger, 1988.

———. "Feast or Famine: Alternative Management Techniques among Periodic-Father Absence Single Career Families." *International Journal of Sociology of the Family* 17, no. 2 (1987): 183–95.

Forsyth, Craig J., and Thomas Marckese. "Thrills and Skills: A Sociological Analysis of Poaching." *Deviant Behavior* 14, no. 2 (1993): 157–72.

Forsyth, Craig, and Marion D. Olivier. "The Theoretical Framing of a Social Problem: Some Conceptual Notes on Satanic Cults." *Deviant Behavior* 11, no. 3 (1990): 281–92.

Forsyth, Craig, and Neal Shover. "No Rest for the Weary . . . Constructing a Problem of Elderly Crime." *Sociological Focus* 19, no. 4 (1986): 375–86.

Fox, Stephen. *John Muir and His Legacy: The American Conservation Movement.* New York: Little and Brown, 1981.

Frank, Andre Gunder. *Latin America: Underdevelopment or Revolution.* New York: Monthly Review Press, 1969.

———. "The Development of Underdevelopment." In *Imperialism and Underdevelopment: A Reader,* edited by Robert Rhodes. New York: Monthly Review Press, 1970.

Gale, Dennis E., and Suzanne Hart. "Who Supports State-Sponsored Growth

Management Programs? Insights from Maine." Paper presented at the annual meeting of the Association of Collegiate Schools of Planning, Austin, Texas, 1990.

Gilmore, Harlan W. "Family-Capitalism in a Community of Rural Louisiana." *Social Forces* 15, no. 1 (1936): 71–75.

———. "Social Isolation of the French Speaking People of Rural Louisiana." *Social Forces* 12, no. 1 (1933): 78–84.

Glaser, Barney G., and Anselm L. Strauss. *The Discovery of Grounded Theory: Strategies for Qualitative Research.* Chicago: Aldine, 1967.

Goffman, Erving. *The Presentation of Self in Everyday Life.* Garden City, N.Y.: Doubleday, 1959.

Goldberg, Robert A. *Grassroots Resistance: Social Movements in Twentieth Century America.* Belmont, Calif.: Wadsworth, 1991.

Goode, William. *World Revolution and Family Patterns.* New York: Free Press, 1963.

Gordon, Raymond L. *Interviewing: Strategy, Techniques, and Tactics.* Homewood, Ill.: Dorsey Press, 1969.

Gorlach, Krzysztof. "The Struggle for Survival: Peasant Movements and Societal Change." *Research in Social Movements, Conflicts, and Change* 10, no. 2 (1988): 161–72.

Gramling, Robert. "Concentrated Work Scheduling: Enabling and Constraining Aspects." *Sociological Perspectives* 32, no. 1 (1989): 47–64.

Gramling, Robert, and Sarah Brabant. "Boom Towns and Offshore Energy Impact Assessment: The Development of a Comprehensive Model." *Sociological Perspectives* 29, no. 2 (1986): 177–201.

Gramling, Robert, and Craig J. Forsyth. "Work Scheduling and Family Interaction." *Journal of Family Issues* 8, no. 2 (1987): 163–75.

Gramling, Robert; Craig J. Forsyth; and Linda Mooney. "The Protestant Ethic and the Spirit of Cajunism." *Journal of Ethnic Studies* 15, no. 1 (1987): 33–46.

Green, Trellis G., and Edward Nissan. "Economic Analysis for Resolving Disputes between Commercial and Recreational Fisheries." Conference on Gulf and South Atlantic Fisheries: Law and Policy. New Orleans, Louisiana: March 18–20, Louisiana Sea Grant and Mississippi-Alabama Sea Grant Consortium, 1987.

Greenpeace. *An Abstract of Waste Management Inc.: An Encyclopedia of Environmental Crimes and Other Misdeeds.* Chicago: Greenpeace, July, 1990.

Griffin, Larry; Joel Devine; and Michael Wallace. "Monopoly Capital, Organized Labor, and Military Expenditure in the United States, 1949–1976." *American Journal of Sociology* 88, supplement (1983a): 113–54.

———. "On the Economic and Political Determinants of Welfare Spending in the Post–World War II Era." *Politics and Society* 12, no. 3 (1983b): 330–70.

Gunter, Valerie J., and Barbara Finlay. "Influences on Group Participation in Environmental Conflicts." *Rural Sociology* 53, no. 4 (1988): 498–505.

Hagen, E. E. *On the Theory of Social Change.* Homewood, Ill.: Dorsey Press, 1962.

Hanna, Susan S., and Courtland L. Smith. "Attitudes of Trawl Vessel Captains about Work, Resource Use, and Fisheries Management." *North American Journal of Fisheries Management* 13 (1993): 367–75.

Harris, Craig K. "Toward a Sociology of Fisheries." *Proceedings of the Workshop on Fisheries Sociology,* edited by Bailey et al. Woods Hole Oceanographic Institution Technical Report WHOI-86-34, April 26–27, 1986.

Hawley, Amos. *Urban Studies: An Ecological Approach.* New York: Ronald Press, 1971.

Hazelrigg, Lawrence E. "Is There a Choice between Constructionism and Objectivism?" *Social Problems* 33, no. 1 (1986): 1–13.

Hearn, Frank. "State Autonomy and Capitalism." *Contemporary Crisis* 8, no. 2 (1984): 125–45.

Heber, R. W. "Fish and Oil: The Cultural Ecology of Offshore Resource Activities in Nova Scotia." In *Fish vs. Oil,* edited by J. D. House. St. John's, Newfoundland: Institute of Social and Economic Research, Memorial University, 1986.

Helfrich, Louis A., and Bernard L. Griswold. 1991. "Public Education in Fisheries: A Review of the Role of Extension." *Reviews in Aquatic Sciences* 4, no. 4 (1991): 317–37.

Henwood, T. A., and W. E. Stuntz. "Analysis of Sea Turtle Captures and Mortalities during Commercial Shrimp Trawling." *Fisheries Bulletin* 85 (1987): 813–17.

Herberle, Rudolf. *Social Movements: An Introduction to Political Sociology.* New York: Appleton-Century-Crofts, 1951.

Hodson, Randy, and Robert L. Kaufman. "Economic Dualism: A Critical Review." *American Sociological Review* 47, no. 6 (1982): 727–39.

Horbulewicz, Jan. "The Parameters of the Psychological Autonomy of Industrial Trawler Crews." In *Seafarer and Community,* edited by Peter H. Fricke. New Jersey: Rowman and Littlefield, 1973.

Horobin, G. W. "Community and Occupation in the Hull Fishing Industry." *British Journal of Sociology* 8, no. 3 (1957): 343–56.

House, J. D. *The Challenge of Oil: Newfoundland's Quest for Controlled Development.* St. John's, Newfoundland: Institute of Social and Economic Research, Memorial University, 1985.

House, J. D., ed. *Fish vs. Oil.* St. John's, Newfoundland: Institute of Social and Economic Research, Memorial University, 1986.

Hughes, E. "Social Changes and Status Protest: An Essay on the Marginal Man." *Phylon* 10, no. 1 (1949): 58–65.

Humphries, Drew. "Serious Crime, News Coverage, and Ideology: A Content Analysis of Crime Coverage in a Metropolitan Paper." *Crime and Delinquency* 27 (April, 1981): 191–205.

Inkeles, Alex. "The Modernization of Man in Socialist and Nonsocialist Countries." In *Social Consequences of Modernization in Communist Societies,* edited by M. G. Fields. Baltimore: Johns Hopkins University Press, 1976.

Jenkins, J. Craig. "Resource Mobilization Theory and the Study of Social Movements." *Annual Reviews of Sociology* 9 (1983): 527–53.

Jessop, Bob. "On Recent Marxist Theories of Law, the State and Juridio-Political Ideology." *International Journal of the Sociology of Law* 8, no. 3 (1980): 339–68.

Johnson, Harry M. *Sociology: A Systematic Introduction.* New York: Harcourt, Brace and World, Inc., 1960.

Kerner Commission. *Report of the National Advisory Commission on Civil Disorders.* New York: Bantam Books, 1968.

Kimeldorf, Howard. "Working Class Culture, Occupational Recruitment, and Union Politics." *Social Forces* 64, no. 2 (1985): 359–76.

Kish, Leslie. *Survey Sampling.* New York: John Wiley and Sons, 1965.

Kitner, Kathi R. TEDS: *A Study of the South Atlantic Shrimp Fishermen's Beliefs, Opinions, and Perceptions Regarding the Use of Turtle Excluder Devices.* Technical Report 5. Charleston, S.C.: South Atlantic Fishery Management Council, 1987.

Klare, Karl. "Law-Making as Praxis." *Telos* 12, no. 2 (1979): 123–35.

Klima, Edward F. "Approaches to Research and Management of U.S. Fisheries for Penaeid Shrimp in the Gulf of Mexico." In *Offprints from Marine Invertebrate Fisheries: Their Assessment and Management,* edited by John F. Caddy. New York: John Wiley and Sons, 1989.

Kroll-Smith, J. Stephen, and Stephen R. Couch. "Sociological Knowledge and the Public at Risk: A 'Still Study' of Sociology, Technological Hazards, and Moral Dilemmas." *Sociological Practice Review* 1, no. 2 (1990): 120–27.

Kuhn, Thomas S. *The Structure of Scientific Revolutions.* Chicago: University of Chicago Press, 1970.

LaPiere, Richard T. *Social Change.* New York: McGraw-Hill, 1965.

Lebon, G. *The Crowd: A Study of the Popular Mind.* New York: Viking Press, 1960.

Lindblom, Charles E. *Politics and Markets.* New York: Basic Books, 1977.

Lipset, Seymour Martin. *Political Man: The Social Basis of Politics.* New York: Doubleday Anchor Books, 1959.

Logan, John R., and Harvey L. Moltoch. *Urban Fortunes: The Political Economy of Place.* Berkeley: University of California Press, 1987.

Lofland, John. *Analyzing Social Settings.* Belmont, Calif.: Wadsworth, 1971.

Lopata, Helen Z. "Social Construction of Social Problems over Time." *Social Problems* 31, no. 3 (1984): 249–72.

Louisiana Cooperative Extension Service. *El Pescador.* Saint Bernard Parish, La.: Louisiana State Agriculture Center, May 10, 1993.

McCarthy, John D., and Mayer N. Zald. "Resource Mobilization and Social

Movements: A Partial Theory." *American Journal of Sociology* 82, no. 5 (1977): 1214–16.

McNamee, Stephen J. "DuPont-State Relations." *Social Problems* 34, no. 1 (1987): 1–17.

Mann, Susan A. "The Rise of Wage Labor in the Cotton South: A Global Analysis." *Journal of Peasant Studies* 14, no. 2 (1987): 226–42.

Mann, Susan, and James M. Dickerson. "Obstacles to the Development of Capitalist Agriculture." *Journal of Peasant Studies* 5, no. 4 (1978): 466–81.

Marchak, Patricia. "The Staples Trap." In Fish vs. Oil, edited by J. D. House. St. John's, Newfoundland: Institute of Social and Economic Research, Memorial University, 1986.

Margavio, A. V.; Shirley Laska; Craig Forsyth; and James Mason. "Captives of Conflict: The TEDS Case." *Journal of Society and Natural Resources* 6 (August, 1993): 273–90.

Marger, Martin N. *Elites and Masses: An Introduction to Political Sociology.* New York: D. Van Nostrand Co., 1981.

———. *Race and Ethnic Relations.* Belmont, Calif.: Wadsworth, 1991.

Maril, Robert Lee. *Texas Shrimpers: Community, Capitalism, and the Sea.* College Station: Texas A&M University Press, 1983.

Merton, R. K. *Social Theory and Social Structure.* New York: Free Press, 1957.

Michalowski, Raymond J., and Ronald C. Kramer. "The Space between Laws: The Problem of Corporate Crime in a Transnational Context." *Social Problems* 34, no. 1 (1987): 34–53.

Miller, Marc; Richard P. Gale; and Perry J. Brown. *Social Science in Natural Resource Management Systems.* Boulder: Westview Press, 1987.

Miller, Morton; Paul J. Hooker; and Peter H. Fricke. "Impressions of Ocean Fisheries Management under the Magnuson Act." Paper presented at the annual meeting of the American Association for the Advancement of Science, New Orleans, Louisiana, February 17, 1990.

Mintz, Beth, and Michael Schwartz. *The Power Structure of American Business.* Chicago: University of Chicago Press, 1985.

Morrison, Denton E. "Some Notes toward Theory on Relative Deprivation, Social Movements, and Social Change." *American Behavioral Scientist* 14, no. 5 (1971): 675–90.

Mott, Paul E. "The Role of the Absentee-Owned Corporation in the Changing Community." In *The Structure of Community Power,* edited by Michael Aiken and Paul E. Mott. New York: Random House, 1970.

National Academy of Science. *Decline of the Sea Turtles: Causes and Prevention.* Washington: National Academy Press, 1990.

National Marine Fisheries. *Fisheries of the United States, 1989.* Washington, D.C.: U.S. Government Printing Office, 1990.

Nisbet, Robert. "The Study of Social Problems" In *Contemporary Social Prob-*

lems, edited by Robert Merton and Robert Nisbet. New York: Harcourt, Brace, Jovanovich, 1971.

O'Connor, James. *The Fiscal Crisis of the State*. New York: St. Martin's Press, 1973.

Offe, Claus. "The Abolition of Market Control and the Problem of Legitimacy." *Kapitalistate* 1, no. 2 (1973): 109–16.

Olmstead, Frederick L. *Cotton Kingdom*. New York: Mason Bros., 1861.

Orbach, M. K. *Hunters, Seamen, and Entrepreneurs: The Tuna Seinermen of San Diego*. Los Angeles: University of California Press, 1977.

Orbach, Michael K., and Jeffrey C. Johnson. "The Transformation of Fishing Communities: A Public Policy Perspective." *Marine Resource Utilization: A Conference on Social Science Issues*. Mobile University of South Alabama College of Arts and Sciences Publication and the Mississippi-Alabama Sea Grant Consortium 1 (1988): 65–70.

Palmer, C. Eddie, and Craig J. Forsyth. "Animals, Attitudes, and Anthropomorphic Sentiment: The Social Construction of Meat and Fur in Postindustrial Society." *International Review of Modern Sociology* 22, no. 1 (1992): 29–44.

Parenton, Vernon J. "Notes on the Social Organization of a French Village in South Louisiana." Social Forces 17, no. 1 (1938): 73–82.

Parsons, Talcott. *Societies: Evolutionary and Comparative Perspectives*. Englwood Cliffs, N.J.: Prentice-Hall, 1966.

Peacock, Walter Gillis; Greg A. Hoover; and Charles D. Killian. "Divergence and Convergence in International Development: A Decomposition Analysis of Inequality in the World System." *American Sociological Review* 53, no. 6 (1988): 838–52.

Pope John XXIII. *Mater et Magistra: Christianity and Social Progress*. New York: America Press, 1961.

Popper, Karl R. *The Logic Of Scientific Inquiry*. London: Hutchinson, 1969.

Poulantzas, Nicos. *Political Power and Social Classes*. London: New Left Books and Sheed and Ward, 1973.

Quadagno, Jill. "Social Movements and State Transformation: Labor and Racial Conflict in the War on Poverty." *American Sociological Review* 57, no. 5 (1992): 616–34.

Reasons, Charles E., and William D. Perdue. *The Ideology of Social Problems*. Sherman Oaks, Calif.: Alfred Publishing Co., 1981.

Reed, N. P., and D. Drabelle. *The United States Fish and Wildlife Service*. Boulder: Westview Press, 1984.

Renaud, Maurice; G. Gitschlas; E. Klima; A. Shah; J. Nance; C. Caillouet; Z. Zein-Eldin; D. Koi; and F. Patella. *Evaluations of the Impacts of Turtle Excluder Devices (TEDs) on Shrimp Catch Rates in the Gulf of Mexico and South Atlantic, March 1988 through July 1989*. National Oceanic and Atmospheric Administration Technical Memorandum NMFSSEFC-254, 1990.

Ritzer, George. *Contempory Sociological Theory.* New York: McGraw-Hill, 1992.

Roberts, Ken. "The Economic Impact of TEDS on the Louisiana Shrimp Fishery." Paper presented at the thirty-first annual meeting of the Louisiana Shrimp Association, New Orleans, Louisiana, 1990.

Ross, Irwin. "Public Relations Isn't Kid Stuff at Mobil." *Fortune* 94 (September, 1976): 110.

Rostow, W. W. *The Stages of Economic Growth: A Non-Communist Manifesto.* Cambridge: Cambridge University Press, 1960.

Schwartz, Frank. Personal correspondence (letter) to Nancy Foster, NMFS national office, July 23, 1990.

Scott, Pam; Evellen Richards; and Brian Martin. "Captives of Controversy: The Myth of the Neutral Social Researcher in Contemporary Scientific Controversies." *Science, Technology, and Human Values* 15 (1990): 474–94.

Seward, Julian H. *The Theory Of Cultural Change.* Urbana: University Of Illinois Press, 1955.

Seydlitz, Ruth; Shirley Laska; Daphne Spain; Elizabeth W. Triche; and Karen Bishop. "Development and Social Problems: The Impact of the Offshore Oil Industry on Suicide and Homicide Rates." *Rural Sociology* 58 (1) 1993: 93–110.

Sheley, Joseph F., and Cindy D. Ashkins. "Crime, Crime News, and Crime Views." *Public Opinion Quarterly* 45 (Winter, 1981): 492–506.

Sinclair, Peter R. "Fisheries and Regional Development: Contradictions of Canadian Policy in the Newfoundland Context." *Proceedings of Marine Resource Utilization: A Conference on Social Science Issues.* Mobile, Ala.: University of South Alabama Publication Service, 1988.

Smelser, Neil S. *Theory of Collective Behavior.* New York: Free Press, 1962.

Smith, C. L. "Intra-Cultural Variation: Decline and Diversity in North Pacific Fisheries." *Human Organization* 35, no. 1 (1976): 55–64.

Smith, T. Lynn, and Vernon J. Parenton. "Acculturation among the Louisiana French." *American Journal of Sociology* 44, no. 3 (1938): 355–64.

Sorokin, Pitirim A. *Society, Culture, and Personality.* New York: Cooper Square Publishers, 1962.

Spain, Daphne. "Been Heres vs. Come Heres: A Theory of Community Change." Paper presented at the annual meeting of the Association of Collegiate Schools of Planning. Austin, Texas, 1990.

Spector, Malcolm, and John Kitsuse. *Constructing Social Problems.* Menlo Park: Cummings, 1977.

Stiles, G. Fishermen. "Wives, Radios: Aspects of Communication in a Newfoundland Fishing Community." In *North Atlantic Fisherman,* edited by R. Anderson and C. Wadel. St. John's, Newfoundland: Memorial University Press, 1972.

Storey, K.; J. Lewis; M. Shrimpton; and D. Clark. *Family Life Adaptations to*

Offshore Oil and Gas Employment. Ottawa, Canada: Environmental Studies Revolving Funds Report, 1986.

Szasz, Andrew. *Ecopopulism: Toxic Wastes and Movements for Environmental Justice.* Minneapolis: University of Minnesota Press, 1994.

Szasz, Thomas. *The Manufacture of Madness.* New York: Delta, 1979.

Thomas, Stephen, and C. M. Formichella. *The Shrimp Processing Industry in Bayou La Batre, Alabama.* Research Report no. 11. Mobile, Ala.: Center for Business and Economic Research, 1987.

Thomas, W. I., and Dorothy Swaine Thomas. *The Child in America.* New York: Knopf, 1928.

Thomas, W. I., and F. Znaniecki. *The Polish Peasant in Europe and America.* 5 vols. Boston: Badger, 1918–20.

Tocqueville, Alexis de. *Democracy in America.* Garden City, N.Y.: Doubleday Anchor Books, 1969.

Tunstall, J. *The Fisherman.* London: MacGibbon and Kee, 1962.

United States Department of Commerce. *Fisheries of the United States.* Washington, D.C.: U.S. Government Printing Office, 1989.

Upton, Harold F.; Peter Hoar; and Melissa Upton. *The Gulf of Mexico Shrimp Fishery: Profile of a Valuable National Resource.* Washington, D.C.: Center for Marine Conservation, 1992.

U.S. Congress. Senate. *Senate Report* No. 100–240, 2702.

Useem, Michael. *Protest Movements in America.* Indianapolis: Bobbs-Merrill, 1975.

Verba, Sidney, and Norman H. Nie. *Participation in America: Political Democracy and Social Equality.* New York: Harper and Row, 1972.

Wallerstein, Immanuel. *The Capitalist World Economy.* Cambridge: Cambridge University Press, 1979.

———. *The Modern World-System: Capitalist Agriculture and the Origins of the European World-Economy in the Sixteenth Century.* New York: Academic Press, 1974.

Watson, John W.; John F. Mitchell; and Arvind K. Shah. "Trawling Efficiency Device: A New Concept for Selective Shrimp Trawling Gear." *Marine Fisheries Review* 48, no. 1 (1986): 19.

Weber, Max. *The Protestant Ethic and the Spirit of Capitalism.* New York: Charles Scribner's Sons, 1958.

White, David R. M. "Sea Turles and Resistance to TEDs among Shrimp Fishermen of the U.S. Gulf Coast." *MAST* 2, no.1 (1989): 69–79.

Williams, T. Harry. *Huey Long.* New York: Knopf, 1969.

Wolf, Eric. *Peasants Wars of the Twentieth Century.* New York: Harper, 1969.

Wolfe, Alan. "New Directions in the Marxist Theory of Politics." *Politics and Society* 4, no. 2 (1974): 131–59.

Woolgar, Steve, and Dorothy Pawluch. "Ontological Gerrymandering: The Anatomy of Social Problems Explanations." *Social Problems* 32, no. 3 (1985): 214–27.

Yaffee, Steven Lewis. *Prohibitive Policy: Implementing the Federal Endangered Species Act.* Cambridge: MIT Press, 1982.

Zald, M. N., and R. Ash. "Social Movement Organizations." *Social Forces* 44, no. 3 (1966): 327–41.

Index

ADM-4781   02/18/97